Ninja Woodfire Pro

Outdoor Grill & Smoker

Cookbook for Beginners

A Super Ninja Woodfire Outdoor Grill & Smoke Recipe Book that Teaches You
Make a Variety of Smoked Flavors with Ease

Kathleen Stenson

Introduction

Are you tired of the endless search for the ideal outdoor electric grill that combines the simplicity of use, easy maintenance, and exceptional woodfire flavor? Are you yearning for a grill that goes beyond basic grilling and adds versatility to your culinary adventures? Look no further. In your quest for the perfect grilling experience, we understand the frustration of finding a grill that meets all your needs. The struggle to balance ease of use, maintenance, and exceptional results can be overwhelming. But fear not, because we have discovered the solution to your grilling woes.

Introducing the 7-in-1 Ninja Woodfire Grill – a culinary marvel that not only grills but also bakes, airfries, dehydrates, and performs a plethora of tasks that elevate your outdoor cooking game to new heights. Imagine having the power to grill succulent steaks, bake perfectly golden bread, airfry crispy fries, and dehydrate your favorite fruits, all with one incredible appliance. The Ninja Woodfire Grill is not just a grill; it's your gateway to a world of culinary possibilities.

As an avid outdoor cooking enthusiast, I was constantly on the lookout for a grill that offered the smoky goodness of woodfire while being user-friendly and multifunctional. When I stumbled upon the Ninja Woodfire Grill, I was skeptical at first, but it quickly surpassed my expectations. The ease with which it grills, bakes, airfries, and more, all while infusing that authentic woodfire flavor, left me awe-struck. It became the heart of my outdoor kitchen, transforming ordinary gatherings into unforgettable feasts.

If you find yourself intrigued by the potential of this extraordinary appliance and are eager to explore its capabilities, you are in the right place. This cookbook is your ticket to unlocking the full potential of your Ninja Woodfire Grill. Within these pages, you will discover a treasure trove of mouthwatering recipes specifically crafted for this versatile grill. Whether you are a seasoned griller or a novice cook, these recipes cater to all skill levels, ensuring that you can create restaurant-quality dishes in the comfort of your own backyard.

So, if you are ready to embark on a culinary adventure like never before, armed with the 7-in-1 Ninja Woodfire Grill and an arsenal of delectable recipes, you are in for a treat. Get ready to savor the tantalizing flavors, aromas, and textures that only a woodfire grill can offer. Your journey to becoming a backyard culinary ninja starts here. Let's fire up those grills and create gastronomic masterpieces together!

What is Ninja Woodfire Outdoor Grill?

This innovative grill redefines outdoor cooking, combining the convenience of electricity with the authentic smoky flavors of real burning wood pellets. With its 3-in-1 functionality as a Master Grill, Foolproof BBQ Smoker, and Outdoor Air Fryer, it offers unmatched versatility, allowing you to grill, smoke, and air fry a wide range of dishes to perfection. Equipped with Ninja Woodfire Technology, this grill infuses your food with rich smoky taste that's visible and delectable. Its user-friendly interface, removable smoke box, and easy-to-clean accessories make outdoor cooking hassle-free, while its weather-resistant design lets you enjoy the grilling experience year-round. Elevate your outdoor cooking adventures with the Ninja Woodfire Outdoor Grill, where convenience meets extraordinary flavor.

The Ninja Woodfire Grill comes with a variety of function buttons, each designed to cater to different cooking styles and techniques. Here's an explanation of the function buttons and their specific uses:

GRILL: This function is used for closed-hood cooking, providing both top and bottom heat. It is ideal for grilling large or thick cuts of meat, frozen food, or when you need an all-around sear on your dishes. Use the closed hood when grilling substantial cuts of meat or frozen foods to ensure even cooking and optimal searing. For delicate foods or lean proteins, you can open the hood to develop char-grilled textures without the risk of overcooking.

SMOKER: The smoker function allows you to create deep, smoky flavors while cooking at low temperatures. It is perfect for tenderizing large cuts of meat and achieving that classic smoky taste. Use the smoker function when you want to cook low and slow, especially for large cuts of meat, to enhance tenderness and infuse a rich smoky flavor.

AIR CRISP: This function is designed to achieve crispiness and crunch in your dishes with little to no oil, utilizing higher fan speeds. It's perfect for making crispy fries, chicken wings, and other fried foods with a healthier twist. Use the air crisp function when you want to enjoy crispy textures without the excess oil. It's great for making healthier versions of your favorite fried foods.

BAKE: The bake function is used for baking cakes, treats, desserts, and more. It operates with lower fan speeds, ensuring that your baked goods are cooked evenly and to perfection. Use the bake function when you want to prepare cakes, cookies, or any other baked treats. The lower fan speeds help in achieving even baking results.

ROAST: The roast function is ideal for tenderizing meats and roasting vegetables. It offers consistent heat to ensure meats are cooked to perfection and vegetables are roasted to a delightful crispness.

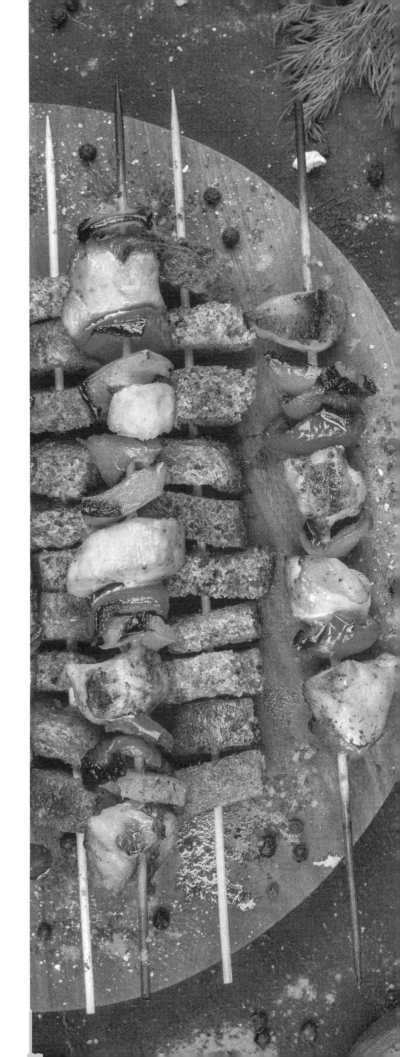

Use the roast function for cooking tender meats and achieving a succulent texture. It's also great for roasting vegetables until they are caramelized and flavorful.

BROIL: The broil function adds a crispy finishing touch to meals. It is perfect for melting cheese on sandwiches or giving your dishes a delightful, crispy exterior.

Use the broil function when you want to achieve a golden, crispy layer on top of your dishes. It's excellent for melting cheese, creating a gratin, or adding a finishing touch to casseroles.

DEHYDRATE: The dehydrate function is used to remove moisture from foods, such as meats, fruits, and vegetables, to create healthy snacks. It preserves the natural flavors and nutrients of the ingredients. Use the dehydrate function when you want to make homemade dried fruits, jerky, or vegetable chips. It's a healthier alternative to store-bought snacks, allowing you to enjoy the natural taste of dehydrated foods.

Operating Buttons

The Ninja Woodfire Grill comes with easy-to-use operating buttons that allow you to control various aspects of the cooking process. Here's a detailed explanation of each button's function:

DIAL: Use the dial to adjust your temperature, cook time, or thermometer settings.

WOODFIRE FLAVOR TECHNOLOGY: Press this button after selecting your cooking function to add Woodfire flavor using the Grill, Air Crisp, Bake, Roast, or Dehydrate functions. When pressed, the flame icon will illuminate on

the display screen, indicating that the Woodfire Flavor Technology is activated.

TEMP (Temperature) Adjustment: The default temperature setting for the selected function will be displayed. Press TEMP to change the grill temperature, use the dial to increase or decrease temperature.

TIME Adjustment: Press TIME to change the cook time, use the dial to increase or decrease time.

START/STOP: Press the START/STOP button to initiate or stop the current cooking function. If you press and hold this button for 4 seconds, it allows you to skip the preheating process for faster cooking initiation.

Preheat for Better Results: For optimal grilling results, it's recommended to let the grill fully preheat before adding food. Preheating ensures even cooking and prevents issues like overcooking, excessive smoke, and longer preheat times. The unit will automatically begin preheating after you set the function, time, and temperature and press START (except when using the Smoker function or the Broil/Dehydrate functions without enabling Woodfire Flavor Technology).

Benefits of Using It

A myriad of benefits to cooking enthusiasts. Its versatility is unparalleled, allowing users to smoke, grill, air crisp, bake, and infuse woodfire flavors, all in one sleek appliance.

Master Grill: With the Ninja Woodfire Grill, you can experience the performance of a full-

size propane grill. It provides the same char and searing capabilities, ensuring your meats and vegetables are cooked to perfection.

Foolproof BBQ Smoker: Creating authentic BBQ bark and flavor is made fast and easy with just ½ cup of pellets. You can achieve that classic smoky taste without the hassle of traditional smokers.

Outdoor Air Fryer: Enjoy the benefits of air frying with a unique twist. The Ninja Woodfire Grill allows you to add a smoky flavor to your air-fried favorites. Additionally, you can cook all your side dishes outdoors, making it a convenient option for preparing complete meals.

Ninja Woodfire Technology: Powered by electricity and flavored by real burning wood pellets, this grill ensures you get 100% real smoky flavor with every cook function. The rich smoky aroma enhances the taste of your dishes, making them truly exceptional. The Ninja Woodfire Grill creates a visually appealing experience with the smoke infusion. Not only can you see the smoke, but you can also taste the difference in your grilled, smoked, and air-fried foods. The grill comes with two blends of 100% real hardwood Ninja Woodfire Pellets. These pellets are designed for flavor, not fuel, ensuring that you only need 1/2 cup to achieve the desired smoky taste in your dishes.

Convenience and Efficiency: The Ninja Woodfire Grill is designed to withstand different

weather conditions, allowing you to cook and store your grill outdoors year-round. Its weather-resistant feature ensures durability and longevity. With a powerful 1760-watt electric system, there's no need for charcoal, propane, or worrying about flare-ups. This makes it balcony and apartment friendly, offering a safe and efficient grilling solution for various living spaces.

Cooking Versatility: Whether you are grilling steaks, hot dogs, air frying wings, or BBQ smoking a whole brisket, the Ninja Woodfire Grill can handle it all. Its large cooking capacity enables you to cook for a crowd, making it ideal for gatherings, parties, and family events.

Step-By-Step Using It

The Ninja Woodfire Grill stands as the epitome of culinary versatility, offering an array of cooking functions that allow enthusiasts to explore their culinary creativity effortlessly. This grill's versatility knows no bounds; it can transform into a powerful smoker, infusing meats with the rich, smoky flavors essential to traditional barbecue.

Grilling

If you are using the Woodfire Flavor Technology, fill the smoke box with Ninja Woodfire Pellets without overflowing. Plug in the grill, select the GRILL function, adjust temperature and cook time settings as desired, and press START for preheating. Once preheating is complete, ADD FOOD will appear on the display. Place ingredients on the grill grate, close the hood, and cooking will commence. When the timer reaches zero, the grill will beep, indicating the cooking is done. Simply open the hood and remove the food from the grill grate.

Smoking

To prepare the smoker, ensure the grill is on a level surface and install the grill grate and grease tray properly. Fill the smoke box with Ninja Woodfire Pellets without overflowing, close the lid, and place the ingredients on the grill grate inside the hood. Plug in the grill, select the SMOKER function by rotating the dial clockwise from the OFF position, adjust the temperature and cook time settings if needed, and press START to begin cooking. Unlike other functions, the smoker doesn't require preheating. When the cook time reaches zero, the grill will beep, displaying END. Open the hood and remove the food from the grill grate.

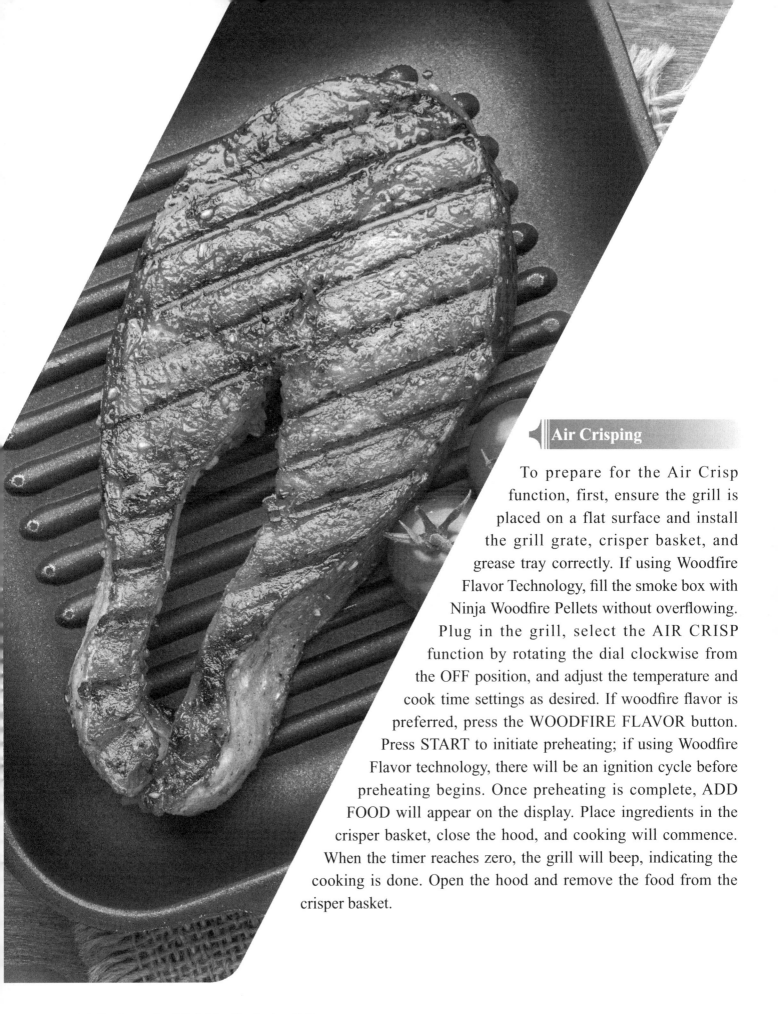

Air Crisping

To prepare for the Air Crisp function, first, ensure the grill is placed on a flat surface and install the grill grate, crisper basket, and grease tray correctly. If using Woodfire Flavor Technology, fill the smoke box with Ninja Woodfire Pellets without overflowing. Plug in the grill, select the AIR CRISP function by rotating the dial clockwise from the OFF position, and adjust the temperature and cook time settings as desired. If woodfire flavor is preferred, press the WOODFIRE FLAVOR button. Press START to initiate preheating; if using Woodfire Flavor technology, there will be an ignition cycle before preheating begins. Once preheating is complete, ADD FOOD will appear on the display. Place ingredients in the crisper basket, close the hood, and cooking will commence. When the timer reaches zero, the grill will beep, indicating the cooking is done. Open the hood and remove the food from the crisper basket.

Baking/ Roasting / Broiling & Dehydrating

To utilize the rest of the functions on compatible models, start by placing the grill on a flat surface and installing the grill grate and grease tray correctly. If opting for the Woodfire Flavor Technology, fill the smoke box with Ninja Woodfire Pellets without overflowing. Ensure the grill is plugged in, then rotate the dial clockwise to select the BAKE/ROAST/BROIL/DEHYDRATE function. Adjust the temperature and cook time settings as needed using the designated buttons. Press START for preheating; if Woodfire Flavor technology is used, the grill will go through an ignition cycle before preheating begins. Once preheating is done, the display will show ADD FOOD. Open the hood and place ingredients directly on the grate or use a bake pan on the grate. Close the hood to initiate cooking, and the timer will count down. When the timer reaches zero, the grill will beep, displaying DONE. Open the hood and remove the food from the grill grate or bake pan.

Tips for Using Accessories

The Ninja Woodfire Grill is not just a standalone appliance; it comes complete with a range of accessories that unlock endless culinary possibilities. These accessories, tailored to the Ninja Woodfire Grill's functions, empower users to experiment, innovate, and create restaurant-quality dishes right in their own kitchens. Mastering these accessories is the key to unlocking the grill's full potential, allowing home cooks to delve into a world of culinary delights.

Grill Grate: The grill grate is the main cooking surface where you place your food. It provides the classic grill marks and allows heat to evenly distribute for proper cooking. It is suitable for grilling various meats, vegetables, and other foods.

Crisper Basket: The crisper basket is designed for air frying. It allows hot air to circulate around the food, making it crispy without the need for excessive oil. It's perfect for preparing items like fries, chicken wings, and other air-fried favorites.

Smoke Box: The smoke box is an essential accessory for the Ninja Woodfire Grill. It holds the wood pellets that create the smoky flavor during cooking. It infuses your dishes with the rich taste of real burning wood, enhancing the overall flavor of grilled, smoked, or air-fried foods.

Grease Tray: The grease tray is placed beneath the grill grate to collect excess grease and drippings from your food. It helps in easy cleanup and prevents flare-ups by keeping the grill's interior clean.

Left and Right Assembly Handles: The left and right assembly handles are used for handling and moving the grill. They provide a secure grip, making it easier to transport the grill or adjust its position as needed.

Socket Head Cap Screw 3.5mm x 16mm (4x) (pre-assembled on handles): These screws are

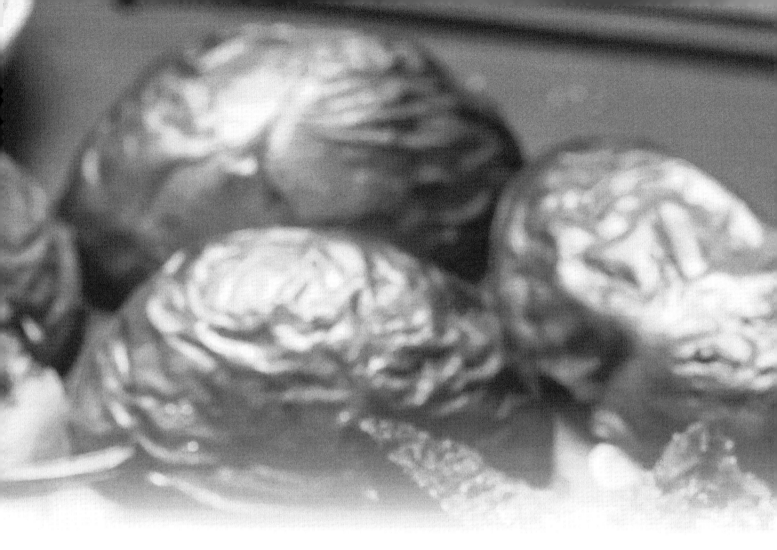

pre-assembled on the handles and are essential for securing the handles to the grill. They ensure the handles are firmly attached, providing stability and safety during use.

Allen Wrench: The Allen wrench is provided for assembling or disassembling the grill if needed. It's used to tighten or loosen the screws, allowing you to adjust or replace components as required.

Pellet Scoop: The pellet scoop is a convenient tool for adding wood pellets to the smoke box. It ensures precise measurements, allowing you to add the right amount of pellets for the desired smoky flavor. Proper usage of the pellet scoop enhances the overall grilling experience.

By utilizing these accessories properly, you can enhance the functionality of your Ninja Woodfire Grill, making it easier to cook a variety of delicious and flavorful dishes.

Straight from the Store

Setting up your Ninja Woodfire Grill after bringing it home from the store involves several important steps to ensure safe and optimal use. Here's a step-by-step guide:

Unboxing and Preparation: Carefully remove all packaging materials, including tapes and accessories, from the unit.

Read the Manual: Read the manual thoroughly, paying close attention to operational instructions, warnings, and important safeguards to prevent injury or property damage.

Cleaning the Accessories: Wash the grill grate and crisper basket in warm, soapy water. Rinse and dry them thoroughly. Note that these accessories are NOT dishwasher safe. NEVER clean the main unit in the dishwasher.

Do not use abrasive brushes or sponges on the cooking surfaces to prevent damage to the coating.

Before First Use: Place all accessories inside the grill. Set the grill to GRILL mode and the temperature to HI. Run the grill for 20 minutes without adding food. This step removes any residues from the manufacturing process. It's safe and won't impact the grill's performance.

Handle Installation: Ensure you are using the correct handle for the left and right sides. The handles are labeled with 'L' and 'R' stickers. Align each handle with the tabs on the base. Push up to set each handle in place.

Use the included Allen wrench to tighten the pre-assembled screws (2x) on each handle to secure them in place.

Extension Cord: Connect the grill to a properly grounded 3-prong GFI outlet. If you need to use an extension cord, make sure it's an outdoor extension cord with a maximum length of 25 feet and no less than 14-gauge. Alternatively, for longer distances, use a 50-foot extension cord with no less than 12-gauge. The cord should be marked with "SJOW" and state that it's suitable for use with outdoor appliances. Using an incorrect cord can lead to overheating, melting, voltage drop, and impact cooking performance.

Install the Smoke Box: To install the smoke box, hold the smoke box lid open with one hand. Insert the removable smoke box carefully into its designated place, ensuring it sits securely in position. To avoid burns, allow the pellets to completely burn out, and let the smoke box cool down entirely. Once the smoke box is cool, remove it carefully from the unit. Safely discard all the contents of the smoke box.

Fill the pellet scoop to the top and level it off to prevent spills. While holding the smoke box lid open, use the pellet scoop to pour the pellets into the smoke box until it's filled to the top. Close the smoke box lid securely. Use only Ninja Woodfire Pellets for the best results, performance, and flavor. Using other types of pellets may affect the taste and overall grilling experience.

Cleaning and Caring for Ninja Woodfire Outdoor Grill

Cleaning your Ninja Woodfire Grill is not just a chore; it's a crucial step in preserving the grill's performance and guaranteeing the impeccable taste of your cooked creations. Regular cleaning prevents the buildup of grease, residue, and

charred particles, which can affect the grill's heat distribution and alter the flavor of your food. By keeping the grill grates, smoke box, crisper basket, and other components clean, you ensure that each dish you prepare benefits from consistent heat and that signature woodfire taste.

Safety First:

- Unplug the Grill: Always unplug the grill from the power source before cleaning. This ensures your safety during the cleaning process.
- Let it Cool: Allow the grill and accessories to cool down after each use. Keeping the hood open helps the unit cool more quickly.

Cleaning the Accessories:

- Smoke Box: Remove the smoke box and safely discard its contents after every use. While cleaning the smoke box is not required, you can use a wire brush to remove extra creosote if desired.
- Pellet Scoop: The pellet scoop is dishwasher safe, so you can clean it in the dishwasher for convenience.
- Grill Grate, Crisper Basket, and Grease Tray: These accessories are not dishwasher safe. Hand-wash them in warm, soapy water after each use. If food residue or grease is stuck, soak the parts in warm, soapy water before cleaning.
- Non-Stick Grill Grate and Crisper Basket: Remove these non-stick accessories after each use and hand-wash them with warm, soapy water.

Cleaning the Inner Hood: Use a damp towel or cloth to wipe down the inside of the hood after each use. This helps deodorize the unit and remove any grease buildup.

Proper Storage:

If you need to stack the coated accessories for storage, place a cloth or paper towel between each piece. This protects the coated surfaces from scratches or damage.

Additional Tips:

Regular cleaning of your Ninja Woodfire Grill is crucial for maintaining its optimal performance. When dealing with stubborn residue, soaking the grill grate or removable parts in warm, soapy water helps loosen stuck-on food and grease. Making cleaning a routine practice after each use ensures the grill remains in good condition, preventing the buildup of grime and ensuring it's ready for the next cooking session. This consistent cleaning routine guarantees the longevity of your grill and ensures it continues to deliver exceptional results whenever you use it.

4-Week Meal Plan

Week 1

Day 1:
Breakfast: Cheesy Zucchini Fritters
Lunch: Simple Smoked Butternut Squash
Snack: Beef Meatballs
Dinner: Roasted Sweet and Sour Pork Chops
Dessert: Delicious Milky Donuts

Day 2:
Breakfast: Homemade French Toasts
Lunch: Coconut Sweet Potatoes & Apple
Snack: Tasty Baked Hush Puppies
Dinner: Simple Crispy Prawns
Dessert: Chocolate Lava Cake

Day 3:
Breakfast: Homemade Burrito
Lunch: Smoky Radicchio with Blue Cheese
Snack: Lime Honey Pineapple
Dinner: Smoked Glazed Ham
Dessert: Baked Pumpkin Streusel Pie Bars

Day 4:
Breakfast: Smoked Trout Frittata
Lunch: Cheesy Tofu with Mushrooms
Snack: Crispy Banana Chips
Dinner: Roasted Herb Whole Chicken
Dessert: Yummy Raisin Bread Pudding

Day 5:
Breakfast: Daily Egg in Bread
Lunch: Baked Spinach and Feta Pita
Snack: Rice Bites with Cheese
Dinner: Grilled Steak with Potato Wedges
Dessert: Stuffed Apples with Sauce

Day 6:
Breakfast: Classic French Toast Sticks
Lunch: Mini Bell Pepper Nachos
Snack: Roasted Crunchy Chickpeas
Dinner: Broiled Salmon with Potatoes
Dessert: Delectable Fruity Crumble

Day 7:
Breakfast: Simple Salmon Ricotta Toast
Lunch: Crispy Zucchini and Yellow Squash
Snack: Homemade Garlic Knots
Dinner: Simple Sweet & Sour Turkey Wings
Dessert: Butter Chocolate Soufflé

Week 2

Day 1:
Breakfast: Cheesy Avocado & Tomato Sandwich
Lunch: Savory Baked Beet Chips
Snack: Homemade Tortilla Chips
Dinner: Herbed Garlic Pork Chops
Dessert: Mini Baked Apple Pies

Day 2:
Breakfast: Tasty Spanish Style Frittata
Lunch: Delicious Marinated Mushrooms
Snack: Mozzarella Crisp Sticks
Dinner: Yummy Crispy Coconut Shrimp
Dessert: Tasty Chocolate Mug Cake

Day 3:
Breakfast: Grilled Breakfast Pancakes
Lunch: Cheesy Beef Burger Balls with Tomatoes
Snack: Easy Broiled Pickles
Dinner: Simple Broiled Lamb Chops
Dessert: Yummy Apple Bread Pudding

Day 4:
Breakfast: Bacon and Bread Cups
Lunch: Rosemary Potato Skins
Snack: Beef Meatballs
Dinner: Garlic Chicken Breasts with Sauce
Dessert: Baked Lemon Bars

Day 5:
Breakfast: Baked Chicken Omelet
Lunch: Rosemary Red Potatoes
Snack: Tasty Baked Hush Puppies
Dinner: Broiled Beef with Potatoes
Dessert: Peach and Berry Pizza

Day 6:
Breakfast: Grilled Savory French Toasts
Lunch: Hasselback Potatoes with Cheese
Snack: Easy Broiled Pickles
Dinner: Honey Salmon Fillet
Dessert: Classic Shortbread Fingers

Day 7:
Breakfast: Green Courgette Fritters
Lunch: Delicious Potato Rosti
Snack: Mozzarella Crisp Sticks
Dinner: Homemade Turkey Burgers
Dessert: Delicious Vanilla Soufflé

Week 3

Day 1:
Breakfast: Breakfast Crispy Bacon
Lunch: Roasted Carrots with Glaze
Snack: Crispy Banana Chips
Dinner: BBQ Roasted Pork Ribs
Dessert: Delicious Milky Donuts

Day 2:
Breakfast: Homemade French Toasts
Lunch: Spicy Potato and Bell Pepper Hash
Snack: Beef Meatballs
Dinner: Garlicky Shrimp with Lemon Juice
Dessert: Delicious Cheesecake

Day 3:
Breakfast: Cheesy Chicken Broccoli Quiche
Lunch: Cheesy Potato Croquettes
Snack: Homemade Tortilla Chips
Dinner: Tandoori Lemon Chicken Legs
Dessert: Baked Pumpkin Streusel Pie Bars

Day 4:
Breakfast: Smoked Trout Frittata
Lunch: Mushrooms with Sesame Seed
Snack: Lime Honey Pineapple
Dinner: Yummy Nut Crusted Rack of Lamb
Dessert: Yummy Raisin Bread Pudding

Day 5:
Breakfast: Cheesy Zucchini Fritters
Lunch: Tasty Stuffed Poblano Peppers
Snack: Rice Bites with Cheese
Dinner: Cheesy Meatballs with Parsley
Dessert: Butter Chocolate Soufflé

Day 6:
Breakfast: Homemade Burrito
Lunch: Baked Spinach and Feta Pita
Snack: Roasted Crunchy Chickpeas
Dinner: Herbed Butter Salmon
Dessert: Stuffed Apples with Sauce

Day 7:
Breakfast: Daily Egg in Bread
Lunch: Coconut Sweet Potatoes & Apple
Snack: Easy Broiled Pickles
Dinner: Thyme Grilled Duck Breasts
Dessert: Delectable Fruity Crumble

Week 4

Day 1:
Breakfast: Classic French Toast Sticks
Lunch: Smoky Radicchio with Blue Cheese
Snack: Homemade Garlic Knots
Dinner: Honey Glazed Pork Shoulder
Dessert: Mini Baked Apple Pies

Day 2:
Breakfast: Tasty Spanish Style Frittata
Lunch: Mini Bell Pepper Nachos
Snack: Mozzarella Crisp Sticks
Dinner: Smoky Lemon Tilapia
Dessert: Tasty Chocolate Mug Cake

Day 3:
Breakfast: Simple Salmon Ricotta Toast
Lunch: Delicious Marinated Mushrooms
Snack: Tasty Baked Hush Puppies
Dinner: French Chicken with Onion
Dessert: Baked Lemon Bars

Day 4:
Breakfast: Cheesy Avocado & Tomato Sandwich
Lunch: Roasted Carrots with Glaze
Snack: Lime Honey Pineapple
Dinner: Homemade Herbed Lamb Chops
Dessert: Classic Shortbread Fingers

Day 5:
Breakfast: Bacon and Bread Cups
Lunch: Crispy Zucchini and Yellow Squash
Snack: Easy Broiled Pickles
Dinner: Beef Stuffed Bell Peppers
Dessert: Yummy Apple Bread Pudding

Day 6:
Breakfast: Grilled Breakfast Pancakes
Lunch: Savory Baked Beet Chips
Snack: Tasty Baked Hush Puppies
Dinner: Crispy Calamari
Dessert: Peach and Berry Pizza

Day 7:
Breakfast: Grilled Savory French Toasts
Lunch: Delicious Marinated Mushrooms
Snack: Rice Bites with Cheese
Dinner: Popcorn Spicy Chicken
Dessert: Delicious Vanilla Soufflé

Chapter 1 Breakfast Recipes

Homemade French Toasts

Prep Time: 10 minutes | Cook Time: 5 minutes | Servings: 2

 Ingredients:

2 eggs
¼ cup evaporated milk
3 tablespoons sugar
2 teaspoons olive oil

⅛ teaspoon vanilla extract
4 bread slices

 **Preparation:**

1. Install the Accessory Frame in the bottom of the oven, then place the Pro-Heat Pan on top of it. 2. In a large bowl, mingle all the ingredients except bread slices. 3. Coat the bread slices evenly with the egg mixture. 4. Arrange the bread slices in the Pro-Heat Pan and close the door. 5. While holding the smoke box open, use the pellet scoop to pour pellets into the smoke box until filled to the top. Then close the smoke box. 6. Turn dial to select SMOKER, set the temperature to 450°F, and set the time to 5 minutes. Select START/STOP to begin cooking. 7. Stirring once in between. 8. Use oven mitts to remove food from the oven. Let it rest, then serve warm.

Serving Suggestions: You can serve it with maple syrup.
Variation Tip: You can also drizzle some cinnamon for added flavor.
Nutritional Information per Serving:
Calories: 261 | Fat: 12g | Sat Fat: 3.6g | Carbohydrates: 30.6g | Fiber: 0.4g | Sugar: 22.3g | Protein: 9.1g

Smoked Trout Frittata

Prep Time: 15 minutes | Cook Time: 20 minutes | Servings: 4

 Ingredients:

2 tablespoons olive oil
1 onion, sliced
6 eggs
½ tablespoon horseradish sauce

2 tablespoons crème Fraiche
2 hot-smoked trout fillets, chopped
¼ cup fresh dill, chopped

 Preparation:

1. Install the Accessory Frame in the bottom of the oven, then place the Pro-Heat Pan on top of it. 2. In a skillet over medium heat, add the oil and onion and sauté for about 5 minutes. 3. Meanwhile, in a bowl, whisk together the eggs, horseradish sauce, dill, trout fillets, and crème Fraiche. 4. Then, transfer the onion mixture into the Pro-Heat Pan. Close the door. 5. While holding the smoke box open, use the pellet scoop to pour pellets into the smoke box until filled to the top. Then close the smoke box. 6. Turn dial to select SMOKER, set the temperature to 450°F, and set the time to 15 minutes. Select START/STOP to begin cooking, flipping once in between. 7. Use oven mitts to remove food from the oven. Let it rest, then serve warm.

Serving Suggestions: Serve with toasted bagels.
Variation Tip: You can also use butter instead of olive oil.
Nutritional Information per Serving:
Calories: 250 | Fat: 18.6g | Sat Fat: 4.1g | Carbohydrates: 4.9g | Fiber: 1g | Sugar: 1.7g | Protein: 16.3g

Cheesy Zucchini Fritters

Prep Time: 5 minutes | Cook Time: 7 minutes | Servings: 8

 **Ingredients:**

10½ ounces zucchini, grated and squeezed
7 ounces Halloumi cheese
¼ cup all-purpose flour

2 eggs
1 teaspoon fresh dill, minced
Salt and black pepper, to taste

 Preparation:

1. Install the Accessory Frame in top level of the oven, then place the Pro-Heat Pan on top of it. 2. Merge together all the ingredients in a large bowl. 3. Make small fritters from this mixture and place them in the Pro-Heat Pan. Close the door. 3. Turn the left-hand dial to select BROIL. Press the TEMP button, then use the right hand dial to set the temp to 360°F. Press the TIME button, then use the right-hand dial to set the time to 7 minutes. Press START/STOP to begin cooking. 4. When cook time is complete, use oven mitts to remove the fritters from the oven and serve warm.

Serving Suggestions: Serve with tomato ketchup.
Variation Tip: You can also use almond flour instead of all-purpose flour.
Nutritional Information per Serving:
Calories: 127 | Fat: 8.6g | Sat Fat: 5.5g | Carbohydrates: 5g | Fiber: 0.5g | Sugar: 1.4g | Protein: 7.6g

Tasty Spanish Style Frittata

Prep Time: 20 minutes | Cook Time: 14 minutes | Servings: 4

 Ingredients:

½ cup frozen corn
½ of chorizo sausage, sliced
1 potato, boiled, peeled and cubed
2 tablespoons feta cheese, crumbled

3 jumbo eggs
1 tablespoon olive oil
Salt and black pepper, to taste

 Preparation:

1. Install the Accessory Frame in the bottom of the oven, then place the Pro-Heat Pan on top of it. 2. In a skillet over medium heat, add chorizo sausage, potato and corn and cook for 6 minutes. 3. In a small bowl, whisk together eggs, salt, and black pepper. 4. Place the sausage mixture into the Pro-Heat Pan and top with the egg mixture and feta cheese. Close the oven door. 5. While holding the smoke box open, use the pellet scoop to pour pellets into the smoke box until filled to the top. Then close the smoke box. 6. Turn dial to select SMOKER, set the temperature to 450°F, and set the time to 8 minutes. Select START/STOP to begin cooking, flipping once in between. 7. When cook time is complete, the oven will beep and DONE will display. Use oven mitts to remove food from the oven. Let it rest and serve warm.

Serving Suggestions: Serve with toasted bagels.
Variation Tip: You can also use baby kale instead of baby spinach.
Nutritional Information per Serving:
Calories: 144 | Fat: 8.5g | Sat Fat: 2.4g | Carbohydrates: 11.5g | Fiber: 1.5g | Sugar: 1.4g | Protein: 6.6g

Homemade Burrito

Prep Time: 15 minutes | Cook Time: 8 minutes | Servings: 2

 **Ingredients:**

2 eggs

2 whole-wheat tortillas

4-ounces chicken breast slices, cooked

¼ of avocado, peeled, pitted and sliced

2 tablespoons mozzarella cheese, grated

2 tablespoons salsa

Salt and black pepper, to taste

 **Preparation:**

1. Install the Accessory Frame in top level of the oven, then place the Pro-Heat Pan on top of it. 2. In a bowl, Whisk the eggs and dust with salt and pepper. 3. Transfer into a non-stick pan. 4. Sauté for about 5 minutes over medium heat and remove eggs from the pan. 5. Divide the eggs in each tortilla, followed by chicken slice, avocado, salsa and mozzarella cheese. 6. Roll up each tortilla tightly and transfer in the Pro-Heat Pan. Close the door. 7. Turn the left-hand dial to select BROIL. Set the temperature to 355°F and set the time to 3 minutes. Press START/STOP to begin cooking. 8. When cook time is complete, use oven mitts to remove food from the oven. Let it rest and serve warm.

Serving Suggestions: Serve with lime and coriander rice.
Variation Tip: You can also make these burritos with corn tortillas.
Nutritional Information per Serving:
Calories: 313 | Fat: 15.9g | Sat Fat: 5.8g | Carbohydrates: 15.2g | Fiber: 3.5g | Sugar: 1.2g | Protein: 29.4g

Daily Egg in Bread

Prep Time: 10 minutes | Cook Time: 10 minutes | Servings: 2

 Ingredients:

2 bread slices

2 eggs

½ tablespoon olive oil

Salt and black pepper, to taste

 **Preparation:**

1. Install the Accessory Frame in the bottom level of the unit. Turn left-hand dial to select BAKE. Set the temperature to 320°F and set the time to 10 minutes. Select START/STOP to begin preheating. 2. Cut a piece from the center of bread slices through a cookie cutter. 3. Place the bread slices on the Pro-Heat Pan after greasing them with olive oil and crack eggs in them. 4. Dust the egg in a bread hole with salt and black pepper. 5. When unit is preheated and ADD FOOD and PRS STRT is displayed, open door, place the pan in the unit. Close the door and select START/ STOP to begin cooking. 6. When cook time is complete, use oven mitts to remove food from the oven. Let it rest and serve warm.

Serving Suggestions: Serve alongside bacon.
Variation Tip: You can use both the white or bran bread.
Nutritional Information per Serving:
Calories: 117 | Fat: 8.2g | Sat Fat: 1.9g | Carbohydrates: 4.9g | Fiber: 0.2g | Sugar: 0.7g | Protein: 6.2g

Classic French Toast Sticks

Prep Time: 10 minutes | Cook Time: 5 minutes | Servings: 4

 Ingredients:

2 tablespoons soft butter
4 bread, sliced into sticks
2 eggs, gently beaten
1 pinch cinnamon

1 pinch ground cloves
Salt, to taste
1 pinch nutmeg

 Preparation:

1. Install the Accessory Frame in top level of the oven, then place the Pro-Heat Pan on top of it. 2. In a large bowl, whisk the eggs with salt, butter, nutmeg, cinnamon, and ground cloves. 3. Dip the breadsticks in the egg mixture and transfer to the Pro-Heat Pan. Close the door. 4. Select BROIL. Set the temperature to 365°F and set the time to 5 minutes. Press START/STOP to begin cooking, stirring once in between. 5. When cook time is complete, use oven mitts to remove food from the oven. Let it rest and serve warm.

Serving Suggestions: You can serve it with maple syrup.
Variation Tip: You can also add margarine instead of butter.
Nutritional Information per Serving:
Calories: 150 | Fat: 8.8g | Sat Fat: 4.5g | Carbohydrates: 13g | Fiber: 0.7g | Sugar: 1.3g | Protein: 4.7g

Simple Salmon Ricotta Toast

Prep Time: 10 minutes | Cook Time: 5 minutes | Servings: 4

 Ingredients:

4 bread slices
8 ounces ricotta cheese
4 ounces smoked salmon
1 shallot, sliced

1 cup arugula
1 garlic clove, minced
1 teaspoon lemon zest
¼ teaspoon black pepper

Preparation:

1. Install the Accessory Frame in top level of the oven, then place the Pro-Heat Pan on top of it. 2. Place the bread slices in the Pro-Heat Pan and close the door. 3. Select BROIL. Set the temperature to 355°F and set the time to 5 minutes. Press START/STOP to begin cooking. 4. When cook time is complete, tossing in between and dish out. 5. In a food processor, combine the ricotta cheese, garlic, and lemon zest and pulse until smooth. Spread this mixture over each bread slice and top with salmon, arugula, and shallot. 6. Sprinkle with black pepper and serve warm.

Serving Suggestions: Serve topped with tomato slices if you desire.
Variation Tip: You can also use whole-wheat bread slices.
Nutritional Information per Serving:
Calories: 144 | Fat: 6g | Sat Fat: 3.1g | Carbohydrates: 9.3g | Fiber: 0.4g | Sugar: 0.7g | Protein: 12.7g

Cheesy Avocado & Tomato Sandwich

Prep Time: 15 minutes | Cook Time: 5 minutes | Servings: 4

 **Ingredients:**

4 sourdough bread slices

2 teaspoons olive oil

2 ounces cheddar cheese, sliced

½ of medium avocado, peeled, pitted and sliced

1 plum tomato, cut into ¼-inch slices

Salt and ground black pepper, as required

2 teaspoons mayonnaise

 **Preparation:**

1. Install the Accessory Frame in the bottom of the oven, then place the Pro-Heat Pan on top of it. 2. Brush one side of each bread slice with the oil. 3. Place 2 bread slices on a work surface, oiled side down. 4. Divide ½ cheese over both slices, followed by the avocado and tomato. 5. Sprinkle with salt and black pepper and top with remaining cheese. 6. Spread the mayonnaise on the inside of the remaining bread slices. 7. Place the mayonnaise coated bread slices on top of the sandwiches, oiled side up. 8. Arrange the sandwiches in the Pro-Heat Pan. Close the door. 9. While holding the smoke box open, use the pellet scoop to pour pellets into the smoke box until filled to the top. Then close the smoke box. 10. Turn dial to select SMOKER, set the temperature to 450°F, and set the time to 5 minutes. Select START/STOP to begin cooking. 11. When the cooking time is completed, open the door and place the sandwiches onto a platter. 12. Cut 2 halves of each sandwich and serve warm.

Serving Suggestions: Serve with ketchup.
Variation Tip: Use real mayonnaise.
Nutritional Information per Serving:
Calories: 194 | Fat: 12.8g | Sat Fat: 4.5g | Carbohydrates: 14.8g | Fiber: 2.5g | Sugar: 1.4g | Protein: 6.6g

Breakfast Crispy Bacon

Prep Time: 1 minutes | Cook Time: 9 minutes | Servings: 6

 **Ingredients:**

6 bacon strips

½ tablespoon olive oil

 **Preparation:**

1. Install the Accessory Frame in top level of the oven, then place the Pro-Heat Pan on top of it. 2. Place the bacon into the pan and drizzle with olive oil. Close the door. 3. Select BROIL. Set the temperature to 350°F and set the time to 9 minutes. Press START/STOP to begin cooking, tossing in between. 4. When cook time is complete, use oven mitts to remove food from the oven. Let it rest and serve warm.

Serving Suggestions: Serve it with half fried egg.
Variation Tip: You can use butter instead of olive oil.
Nutritional Information per Serving:
Calories: 110 | Fat: 10.2g | Sat Fat: 3.2g | Carbohydrates: 0g | Fiber: 0g | Sugar: 0g | Protein: 4g

Grilled Breakfast Pancakes

Prep Time: 15 minutes | Cook Time: 8 minutes | Servings: 8

 Ingredients:

1½ teaspoons baking powder
1½ cups all-purpose flour
3 teaspoons sugar, granulated
1 large egg

2 tablespoons unsalted butter, melted
¼ teaspoon kosher salt
1½ cups buttermilk

 Preparation:

1. Install the Accessory Frame in the bottom of the oven, then place the Pro-Heat Pan on top of it. 2. In a bowl, mix together the flour, sugar, baking powder, and salt. 3. In another bowl, whisk in the egg, buttermilk, and butter. 4. Fold the egg mixture thoroughly in the flour mixture. 5. Place the pancake mixture in the Pro-Heat Pan and close the door. 6. While holding the smoke box open, use the pellet scoop to pour pellets into the smoke box until filled to the top. Then close the smoke box. 7. Turn dial to select SMOKER, set the temperature to 450°F, and set the time to 8 minutes. Select START/STOP to begin cooking, flipping once in between. 8. When cooking is complete, use oven mitts to remove the pancake from the oven. Let it rest and serve warm.

Serving Suggestions: Serve drizzled with maple syrup.
Variation Tip: You can also use coconut flour instead of all-purpose flour.
Nutritional Information per Serving:
Calories: 145 | Fat: 4.1g | Sat Fat: 2.3g | Carbohydrates: 22.1g | Fiber: 0.7g | Sugar: 3.8g | Protein: 4.8g

Bacon and Bread Cups

Prep Time: 10 minutes | Cook Time: 15 minutes | Servings: 6

 Ingredients:

6 bread slices
6 bacon slices
1 scallion, chopped

6 eggs
3 tablespoons green bell pepper, seeded and chopped
2 tablespoons low-fat mayonnaise

 Preparation:

1. Install the Accessory Frame in the bottom level of the unit. Turn left-hand dial to select BAKE. Set the temperature to 375°F and set the time to 15 minutes. Select START/STOP to begin preheating. 2. Place each bacon slice in a prepared muffin cup. 3. Cut the round bread slices with a cookie cutter and place over the bacon slices. 4. Top evenly with bell pepper, scallion, and mayonnaise and crack 1 egg in each muffin cup. 5. Place these cups in the Pro-Heat Pan. 6. When unit is preheated and ADD FOOD and PRS STRT is displayed, open the door, place the pan in the unit. Close the door and select START/ STOP to begin cooking. 7. Serve and enjoy!

Serving Suggestions: Serve topped with cherry tomatoes
Variation Tip: You can also use red or yellow bell pepper.
Nutritional Information per Serving:
Calories: 229 | Fat: 14.4g | Sat Fat: 4.3g | Carbohydrates: 11g | Fiber: 1.1g | Sugar: 4.1g | Protein: 14g

Grilled Savory French Toasts

Prep Time: 10 minutes | Cook Time: 7 minutes | Servings: 2

 **Ingredients:**

¼ cup chickpea flour
3 tablespoons onion, finely chopped
2 teaspoons green chili, seeded and finely chopped
Water, as required
4 bread slices

½ teaspoon red chili powder
¼ teaspoon ground turmeric
¼ teaspoon ground cumin
Salt, to taste

Preparation:

1. Install the Accessory Frame in the bottom of the oven, then place the Pro-Heat Pan on top of it. 2. In a large bowl, mingle all the ingredients except bread slices. 3. Coat the bread slices evenly with egg mixture. 4. Arrange the bread slices in the Pro-Heat Pan and close the door. 5. While holding the smoke box open, use the pellet scoop to pour pellets into the smoke box until filled to the top. Then close the smoke box. 6. Turn dial to select SMOKER, set the temperature to 450°F, and set the time to 7 minutes. Select START/STOP to begin cooking, flipping once in between. 7. When cook time is complete, use oven mitts to remove food from the oven. Let it rest and serve warm.

Serving Suggestions: Serve with green mint dip.
Variation Tip: You can increase or decrease spices as per your taste.
Nutritional Information per Serving:
Calories: 151 | Fat: 2.3g | Sat Fat: 0.3g | Carbohydrates: 26.7g | Fiber: 5.4g | Sugar: 4.3g | Protein: 6.5g

Baked Chicken Omelet

Prep Time: 10 minutes | Cook Time: 16 minutes | Servings: 2

 **Ingredients:**

1 teaspoon butter
1 onion, chopped
½ jalapeño pepper, seeded and chopped

3 eggs
¼ cup chicken, cooked and shredded
Salt and black pepper

Preparation:

1. Install the Accessory Frame in the bottom level of the unit. Turn left-hand dial to select BAKE. Set the temperature to 350°F and set the time to 10 minutes. Select START/STOP to begin preheating. 2. In a skillet over medium heat, add butter and onion and sauté for 5 minutes. 3. Add jalapeño pepper and sauté for 1 minute. 4. Stir in the chicken and dish it out into a plate. 5. Meanwhile, in a bowl, whisk together the eggs, salt, and black pepper. 6. Place the chicken mixture in the Pro-Heat Pan. 7. When unit is preheated and ADD FOOD and PRS STRT is displayed, open door, place the pan in the unit. Close the door and select START/ STOP to begin cooking, flipping once in between. 8. When cook time is complete, use oven mitts to remove food from the oven. Let it rest and serve warm.

Serving Suggestions: Serve with browned toast slices.
Variation Tip: You can also add mozzarella and cheddar cheese.
Nutritional Information per Serving:
Calories: 161 | Fat: 9.1g | Sat Fat: 3.4g | Carbohydrates: 5.9g | Fiber: 1.3g | Sugar: 3g | Protein: 19g

Green Courgette Fritters

Prep Time: 15 minutes | Cook Time: 7 minutes | Servings: 2

 Ingredients:

½ teaspoon sea salt
½ teaspoon baking powder
4½ oz. courgette, coarsely grated
1 large free-range egg

3 tablespoons plain flour
2 ounces frozen peas, thawed
Black pepper, to taste
1½ teaspoons ground cumin

 Preparation:

1. Install the Accessory Frame in top level of the oven, then place the Pro-Heat Pan on top of it. 2. In a large bowl, mix together all the ingredients. 3. Make small fritters from this mixture and place them in the pan. Close the door. 4. Select BROIL. Set the temperature to 360°F and set the time to 7 minutes. Press START/STOP to begin cooking. 5. When cook time is complete, use oven mitts to remove food from the oven. Let it rest and serve warm.

Serving Suggestions: Serve with mango yogurt chutney.
Variation Tip: You can also add use zucchini in this recipe.
Nutritional Information per Serving:
Calories: 143 | Fat: 2g | Sat Fat: 0.2g | Carbohydrates: 26g | Fiber: 5.7g | Sugar: 6.6g | Protein: 9g

Cheesy Chicken Broccoli Quiche

Prep Time: 10 minutes | Cook Time: 12 minutes | Servings: 8

 Ingredients:

1 frozen ready-made pie crust
1 egg
⅓ cup cheddar cheese, grated
¼ cup boiled broccoli, chopped
¼ cup cooked chicken, chopped

½ tablespoon olive oil
3 tablespoons whipping cream
Salt to taste
Pepper to taste

 Preparation:

1. Install the Accessory Frame in the bottom of the oven, then place the Pro-Heat Pan on top of it. 2. In a bowl, whisk the egg with whipping cream, salt, cheese, and black pepper. 3. Arrange pie in the greased Pro-Heat Pan and press in the bottom and sides gently and pour the egg mixture over pie crust. 4. Spread the chicken and broccoli on top. 5. Place the pan in the unit and close the door. 6. While holding the smoke box open, use the pellet scoop to pour pellets into the smoke box until filled to the top. Then close the smoke box. 7. Turn dial to select SMOKER, set the temperature to 450°F, and set the time to 12 minutes. Select START/STOP to begin cooking. 8. Serve warm and enjoy.

Serving Suggestions: Served with chopped cilantro on top.
Variation Tip: You can use simple cream instead of whipping cream.
Nutritional Information per Serving:
Calories: 140 | Fat: 10g | Sat Fat: 3.2g | Carbohydrates: 8.3g | Fiber: 0.2g | Sugar: 0.8g | Protein: 4g

Chapter 2 Vegetable and Sides Recipes

Coconut Sweet Potatoes & Apple

Prep Time: 10 minutes | Cook Time: 45 minutes | Servings: 4

 Ingredients:

4 medium sweet potatoes
½ cup coconut Greek yogurt

1 medium apple, chopped
¼ cup toasted coconut flake

 Preparation:

1. Install the Accessory Frame in the bottom level of the unit. Turn left-hand dial to select BAKE. Set the temperature to 400°F and set the time to 45 minutes. Select START/STOP to begin preheating. 2. Arrange sweet potatoes in the Pro-Heat Pan. 3. When unit is preheated and ADD FOOD and PRS STRT is displayed, open the door, place the pan in the unit. Close the door and select START/ STOP to begin cooking. 4. When cook time is complete, cut an "X" in each sweet potato using a sharp knife. Then, fluff the pulp with a fork. Top with the remaining ingredients. 5. Serve and enjoy!

Serving Suggestions: Top with maple syrup.
Variation Tip: You can skip apples.
Nutritional Information per Serving:
Calories: 321 | Fat: 3g | Sat Fat: 2g | Carbohydrates: 70g | Fiber: 8g | Sugar: 30g | Protein: 7g

Simple Smoked Butternut Squash

Prep Time: 5 minutes | Cook Time: 8 minutes | Servings: 4

 Ingredients:

4 cups butternut squash, peeled, and small diced
1 teaspoon olive oil

Salt and pepper to taste

 Preparation:

1. Wash and carefully cut the butternut squash into workable pieces. 2. Cut the squash into small cubes. 3. Using a peeler or a knife, peel all of the squash. 4. Clean the seeds out of the bottom pieces using a big spoon. Remove the seed guts and throw them away. 5. Install the Accessory Frame in the bottom of the oven, then place the Pro-Heat Pan on top of it. 6. Arrange the butternut squash in the pan and shower with olive oil. Sprinkle salt and pepper. Close the door. 7. While holding the smoke box open, use the pellet scoop to pour pellets into the smoke box until filled to the top. Then close the smoke box. 8. Turn dial to select SMOKER, set the temperature to 450°F, and set the time to 8 minutes. Select START/STOP to begin cooking, turning them occasionally. 9. Place on a serving plate. Serve and enjoy!

Serving Suggestions: Serve with steaks.
Variation Tip: Add 1-2 tablespoons of brown sugar on top of the cooked squash.
Nutritional Information per Serving:
Calories: 184 | Fat: 3g | Sat Fat: 0g | Carbohydrates: 43g | Fiber: 13g | Sugar: 8g | Protein: 4g

Baked Spinach and Feta Pita

Prep Time: 10 minutes | Cook Time: 12 minutes | Servings: 6

 **Ingredients:**

6 ounces sun-dried tomato pesto
6 whole wheat pita bread
2 plum tomatoes, chopped
1 bunch of spinach, rinsed and chopped
4 fresh mushrooms, sliced

½ cup crumbled feta cheese
2 tablespoons grated Parmesan cheese
3 tablespoons olive oil
Ground black pepper, to taste

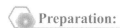 **Preparation:**

1. Install the Accessory Frame in the bottom level of the unit. Turn left-hand dial to select BAKE. Set the temperature to 350°F and set the time to 12 minutes. Select START/STOP to begin preheating. 2. Spread tomato pesto on one side of each pita bread and set it on Pro-Heat Pan. 3. In a bowl, toss the tomatoes, mushrooms, spinach, feta cheese, and Parmesan cheese on top of the pitas. Drizzle with olive oil and season with pepper. 4. When unit is preheated and ADD FOOD and PRS STRT is displayed, open the door, place the pan in the unit. Close the door and select START/ STOP to begin cooking. 5. Once done, cut pitas into quarters. Serve and enjoy!

Serving Suggestions: Top with chopped cilantro.
Variation Tip: You can use any tomatoes.
Nutritional Information per Serving:
Calories: 349 | Fat: 17g | Sat Fat: 3.9g | Carbohydrates: 41g | Fiber: 6.9g | Sugar: 2.8g | Protein: 11g

Cheesy Tofu with Mushrooms

Prep Time: 15 minutes | Cook Time: 10 minutes | Servings: 8

 **Ingredients:**

8 tablespoons Parmesan cheese, shredded
2 cups fresh mushrooms, finely chopped
2 blocks tofu, pressed and cubed into 1-inch pieces

Salt and black pepper, to taste
8 tablespoons butter

Preparation:

1. Install the Accessory Frame in top level of the oven, then place the Pro-Heat Pan on top of it. 2. In a bowl, season the tofu with salt and black pepper. 3. Put butter and tofu in a pot and sauté for 5 minutes. 4. Add mushrooms and Parmesan cheese and sauté for 3 minutes. 5. Place the tofu mixture in the Pro-Heat Pan and close the door. 6. Select BROIL. Set the temperature to 350°F and set the time to 2 minutes. Press START/STOP to begin cooking. 7. When cooking is complete, dole out in a platter to serve warm.

Serving Suggestions: Serve with tortillas.
Variation Tip: You can add any tasteful variety of mushrooms.
Nutritional Information per Serving:
Calories: 142 | Fat: 13.9g | Sat Fat: 8.5g | Carbohydrates: 1.2g | Fiber: 0.4g | Sugar: 0.4g | Protein: 4.6g

Smoky Radicchio with Blue Cheese

Prep Time: 10 minutes | Cook Time: 8 minutes | Servings: 4

Ingredients:

3 tablespoons olive oil, divided
2 tablespoons white balsamic vinegar
½ teaspoon Dijon mustard
Salt and pepper to taste

1 head radicchio
2 tablespoons coarsely chopped pistachio nuts
2 tablespoons crumbled blue cheese

Preparation:

1. In a bowl, combine the balsamic vinegar, olive oil, Dijon mustard, salt, and black pepper. Set aside the dressing. 2. Cut the radicchio head into four wedges with a sharp knife. Brush the wedges with the 1 tablespoon of olive oil and sprinkle with a pinch of salt. 3. Then place them in the Pro-Heat Pan and shower with olive oil. 4. Install the Accessory Frame in the bottom of the oven, then place the Pro-Heat Pan on top of it. Close the door. 5. While holding the smoke box open, use the pellet scoop to pour pellets into the smoke box until filled to the top. Then close the smoke box. 6. Turn dial to select SMOKER, set the temperature to 450°F, and set the time to 8 minutes. Select START/STOP to begin cooking, turning them occasionally. 7. When cook time is complete, drizzle the dressing over the salad and sprinkle it with pistachios and blue cheese. Serve and enjoy!

Serving Suggestions: Serve with fries.
Variation Tip: You can use white wine instead of vinegar.
Nutritional Information per Serving:
Calories: 144 | Fat: 13g | Sat Fat: 2.4g | Carbohydrates: 4.7g | Fiber: 0.9g | Sugar: 1.7g | Protein: 2.5g

Savory Baked Beet Chips

Prep Time: 15 minutes | Cook Time: 15 minutes | Servings: 4

Ingredients:

6-8 medium large beets
Olive oil

1 tablespoon flaked sea salt
1 tablespoon dried chives

Preparation:

1. Install the Accessory Frame in the bottom level of the unit. Turn left-hand dial to select BAKE. Set the temperature to 400°F and set the time to 15 minutes. Select START/STOP to begin preheating. 2. Remove the greens and roots from the beets. Scrub the beets well under cold water. Cut into 1/16" thick slices of beets. 3. Arrange them in the Pro-Heat Pan and drizzle with olive oil. 4. When unit is preheated and ADD FOOD and PRS STRT is displayed, open the door, place the pan in the unit. Close the door and select START/ STOP to begin cooking. 5. Meanwhile, crumble the dried chives into salt. Let beets to cool when cooking is complete. 6. Then, transfer to a cooling rack to finish drying and crisping. 7. Sprinkle with the chive salt. Serve and enjoy!

Serving Suggestions: Sprinkle pepper on top.
Variation Tip: You can also fry them instead of bake.
Nutritional Information per Serving:
Calories: 71 | Fat: 0.3g | Sat Fat: 0g | Carbohydrates: 15g | Fiber: 4g | Sugar: 11g | Protein: 2g

Mini Bell Pepper Nachos

Prep Time: 5 minutes | Cook Time: 10 minutes | Servings: 4

 **Ingredients:**

¼ cup jalapeno pepper, diced
Cooking spray
1 can chicken breast, drained
½ cup avocado, mashed
½ cup plain Greek yogurt

2 cups cheddar cheese, shredded, divided
1 teaspoon chili powder
24 mini bell peppers, halved with stem, seeds and
membranes removed
¼ cup scallions, chopped

 **Preparation:**

1. Install the Accessory Frame in the bottom level of the unit. Turn left-hand dial to select BAKE. Set the temperature to 350°F and set the time to 5 minutes. Select START/STOP to begin preheating. 2. Heat a greased pan and sauté the jalapeno until tender. 3. In a bowl, add chicken, avocado, jalapeno, cheese, yogurt, and chili powder and mix well. 4. Place bell peppers in the Pro-Heat Pan, fill them with chicken mixture, and add some cheese. 5. When unit is preheated and ADD FOOD and PRS STRT is displayed, open the door, place the pan in the unit. Close the door and select START/ STOP to begin cooking. 6. When cook time is complete, sprinkle with chopped scallions and serve.

Serving Suggestions: Serve with salsa.
Variation Tip: You can also use parmesan cheese instead of cheddar.
Nutritional Information per Serving:
Calories: 330 | Fat:.13g | Sat Fat: 7.1g | Carbohydrates: 21g | Fiber: 3.4g | Sugar: 2.1g | Protein: 21g

Rosemary Potato Skins

Prep Time: 5 minutes | Cook Time: 20 minutes | Servings: 2

 **Ingredients:**

2 medium russet potatoes
cooking spray

1 tablespoon minced fresh rosemary
⅛ teaspoon freshly ground black pepper

 **Preparation:**

1. Pierce the potatoes with a fork and place them in the Pro-Heat Pan. 2. Install the Accessory Frame in the bottom of the oven, then place the Pro-Heat Pan on top of it. Close the door. 3. Select BROIL. Set the temperature to 375°F and set the time to 10 minutes. Press START/STOP to begin cooking, tossing them in between. 4. When cook time is complete, halve the potatoes and scrape the pulp, leaving some potato flesh attached to the skin. Save the pulp. 5. Coat each potato skin with cooking spray. 6. Combine the rosemary, pepper and potato flesh in a small bowl; stir well. 7. Place them in the potato skins. Put the skins back and cook for 5 to 10 minutes. Serve right away.

Serving Suggestions: Serve with sauce.
Variation Tip: You can also add chili flakes on top.
Nutritional Information per Serving:
Calories: 50 | Fat: 2g | Sat Fat: 2g | Carbohydrates: 10g | Fiber: 4g | Sugar: 1g | Protein:2g

Delicious Marinated Mushrooms

Prep Time: 5 minutes | Cook Time: 8 minutes | Servings: 4

 Ingredients:

2 large portobello mushrooms
2 tablespoons olive oil
1 tablespoon red wine vinegar

¼ teaspoon salt
¼ teaspoon black pepper

 Preparation:

1. Drizzle olive oil over the mushroom cap, then season with salt, black pepper, and vinegar. 2. Marinate for 30 minutes in the refrigerator. 3. Install the Accessory Frame in the bottom of the oven, then place the Pro-Heat Pan on top of it. 4. Arrange the mushrooms in the pan and shower with olive oil. Close the door. 5. While holding the smoke box open, use the pellet scoop to pour pellets into the smoke box until filled to the top. Then close the smoke box. 6. Turn dial to select SMOKER, set the temperature to 450°F, and set the time to 8 minutes. Select START/STOP to begin cooking, turning them occasionally. 7. Serve and enjoy!

Serving Suggestions: Serve hot with some spicy sauce.
Variation Tip: You can use any oil.
Nutritional Information per Serving:
Calories: 96 | Fat: 10g | Sat Fat: 3g | Carbohydrates: 1g | Fiber: 1g | Sugar: 1g | Protein: 1g

Rosemary Red Potatoes

Prep Time: 5 minutes | Cook Time: 10 minutes | Servings: 4

 Ingredients:

1 pound red potatoes, quartered
8 large garlic cloves, smashed
3 large sprigs of rosemary

2 tablespoons unsalted butter
Salt & pepper, to taste
Olive oil

 Preparation:

1. Install the Accessory Frame in the bottom level of the unit. Turn left-hand dial to select BAKE. Set the temperature to 350°F and set the time to 5 minutes. Select START/STOP to begin preheating. 2. In a large mixing bowl, toss the red potatoes with a pinch of salt and pepper, and 1-2 tablespoons of olive oil. 3. Place the red potatoes in the Pro-Heat Pan. 4. When unit is preheated and ADD FOOD and PRS STRT is displayed, open the door, place the pan in the unit. Close the door and select START/ STOP to begin cooking. 5. After 5 minutes, add all of the remaining ingredients and toss well. Bake for another 4-5 minutes. 6. Remove the potatoes when they are thoroughly cooked and serve them hot. 7. Serve and enjoy!

Serving Suggestions: Serve with steak.
Variation Tip: You can add red chili flakes.
Nutritional Information per Serving:
Calories: 134 | Fat: 6.2g | Sat Fat: 3g | Carbohydrates: 18g | Fiber: 2g | Sugar: 1g | Protein: 2.2g

Cheesy Beef Burger Balls with Tomatoes

Prep Time: 10 minutes | Cook Time: 18 minutes | Servings: 4

 **Ingredients:**

1 lb. lean ground beef
¼ cup onion, finely chopped
1 clove garlic, minced
1 tablespoon mustard
½ teaspoon salt

4 slices of cheddar cheese, chopped
24 dill pickle chips
4 large green lettuce leaves, torn into small pieces
12 cherry tomatoes

Preparation:

1. Install the Accessory Frame in the bottom level of the unit. Turn left-hand dial to select BAKE. Set the temperature to 350°F and set the time to 15 minutes. Select START/STOP to begin preheating. 2. In a bowl, mix together the beef, onion, mustard sauce, garlic, and salt. Make small balls from this mixture. Then place the balls in the Pro-Heat Pan. 3. When unit is preheated and ADD FOOD and PRS STRT is displayed, open the door, place the pan in the unit. Close the door and select START/ STOP to begin cooking. 4. When cook time is complete, top with cheese and bake for more 3 minutes until cheese melts. 5. Layer pickle chip, lettuce, and tomato on a toothpick and place on each meatball. Serve.

Serving Suggestions: Top with cream cheese.
Variation Tip: You can also add spring onions.
Nutritional Information per Serving:
Calories: 307 | Fat:.19.9g | Sat Fat: 7.2g | Carbohydrates: 20.3g | Fiber: 4.5g | Sugar: 7.8g | Protein: 30.1g

Crispy Zucchini and Yellow Squash

Prep Time: 5 minutes | Cook Time: 10 minutes | Servings: 8

 **Ingredients:**

4 tablespoons avocado oil
2 small zucchinis, sliced
1 small yellow squash, sliced

1 tablespoon Sasquatch BBQ Moss
1 teaspoon flaky salt
¼ teaspoon freshly cracked pepper

Preparation:

1. Install the Accessory Frame in top level of the oven, then place the Pro-Heat Pan on top of it. 2. Wash the vegetables and slice them into ¼-inch thick circles. 3. Arrange them in the pan and add the oil on top. Close the door. 4. Select BROIL. Set the temperature to 375°F and set the time to 10 minutes. Press START/STOP to begin cooking, tossing them in between. 5. When done, sprinkle salt and pepper on top. Toss with BBQ Moss. 6. Serve and enjoy!

Serving Suggestions: Sprinkle with a little additional Moss.
Variation Tip: You can use any oil.
Nutritional Information per Serving:
Calories: 76 | Fat: 7g | Sat Fat: 1g | Carbohydrates: 3g | Fiber: 1g | Sugar: 2g | Protein: 1g

Mushrooms with Sesame Seed

Prep Time: 10 minutes | Cook Time: 8 minutes | Servings: 6

 Ingredients:

1½ pounds mixed mushrooms
Extra-virgin olive oil for drizzling
Kosher salt and pepper, to taste

1 tablespoon toasted sesame seeds
2 teaspoons mirin
2 teaspoons soy sauce

 Preparation:

1. Clean the mushrooms. Slice large button or cremini mushrooms into ½-inch thick. Cut the others. 2. Toss the mushrooms in a large mixing bowl with olive oil to coat. Season with salt and pepper. Arrange mushrooms in the Pro-Heat Pan. 3. Install the Accessory Frame in top level of the oven, then place the Pro-Heat Pan on top of it. 4. Select BROIL. Set the temperature to 325°F and set the time to 8 minutes. Press START/STOP to begin cooking, tossing them in between. 5. When cook time is complete, dole out on a platter. 6. In a small bowl, mix the mirin, sesame seeds, and soy sauce. Remove the mushrooms and serve with the sesame dressing.

Serving Suggestions: Sprinkle sesame on top.
Variation Tip: You can also add paprika.
Nutritional Information per Serving:
Calories: 206 | Fat: 17g|Sat Fat: 7g|Carbohydrates: 9g|Fiber: 4g|Sugar: 5g|Protein: 6g

Delicious Potato Rosti

Prep Time: 15 minutes | Cook Time: 10 minutes | Servings: 2

 Ingredients:

1 teaspoon olive oil
½ pound russet potatoes, peeled and roughly grated
1 tablespoon fresh chives, finely chopped

Salt and black pepper, as required
2 tablespoons sour cream
3½ ounces smoked salmon, cut into slices

 Preparation:

1. Install the Accessory Frame in the bottom of the oven. 2. In a large bowl, toss the potatoes with chives, salt, and black pepper. 3. Place the potato mixture in the Pro-Heat Pan. Place the pan in the unit and close the door. 4. While holding the smoke box open, use the pellet scoop to pour pellets into the smoke box until filled to the top. Then close the smoke box. 5. Turn dial to select SMOKER, set the temperature to 400°F, and set the time to 10 minutes. Select START/STOP to begin cooking, tossing once in between. 6. Dole out in a plate when cooked completely, serve after cutting them into wedges and topping them with the sour cream and smoked salmon slices.

Serving Suggestions: Serve topped with the sour cream and smoked salmon slices.
Variation Tip: You can use red potatoes too.
Nutritional Information per Serving:
Calories: 183| Fat: 7.1g|Sat Fat: 2.4g|Carbohydrates: 18.4g|Fiber: 2.8g|Sugar: 1.4g|Protein: 11.4g

Spicy Potato and Bell Pepper Hash

Prep Time: 5 minutes | Cook Time: 7 minutes | Servings: 3

 Ingredients:

5 russet potatoes, peeled and cubed
2 cups water
½ tablespoon extra-virgin olive oil
½ jalapeño, chopped
½ green bell pepper, seeded and chopped
¼ tablespoon dried oregano, crushed

¼ tablespoon ground cumin
Salt and black pepper, to taste
½ onion, chopped
½ red bell pepper, seeded and chopped
¼ tablespoon garlic powder
¼ tablespoon red chili powder

Preparation:

1. Install the Accessory Frame in top level of the oven, then place the Pro-Heat Pan on top of it. 2. In a large bowl filled with water, soak the potatoes for about 30 minutes. 3. Drain well and pat them dry with paper towels. 4. In a bowl, toss the potatoes with oil until well coated. 5. Then transfer the potatoes to the Roast Rack. Place the Roast Rack in the Pro-Heat Pan and close the door. 6. Select BROIL. Set the temperature to 425°F and set the time to 5 minutes. Press START/STOP to begin cooking, tossing once in between. 7. Dish out the potatoes in a bowl and mash well. 8. Add rest of the ingredients and toss well. 9. Broil them in the oven again for 2 minutes at 350°F. Serve warm.

Serving Suggestions: Serve inside the buns.
Variation Tip: You can use pork, chicken, or beef sausages as required.
Nutritional Information per Serving:
Calories: 293| Fat: 3.1g|Sat Fat: 0.5g|Carbohydrates: 62g|Fiber: 10g|Sugar: 7.2g|Protein: 6.9g

Roasted Carrots with Glaze

Prep Time: 10 minutes | Cook Time: 33 minutes | Servings: 4

 Ingredients:

For Glaze:
¼ cup honey
¼ cup soy sauce
1 tablespoon brown sugar
For Carrots:
3 large carrots, peeled and cut into pieces
2 tablespoons extra-virgin olive oil

1 teaspoon minced garlic, about 1 medium clove
½ teaspoon fresh ginger, grated
¼ teaspoon red pepper flakes, crushed

1 scallion, thinly sliced
salt, to taste

Preparation:

1. To make the glaze, in a small bowl, mix honey, brown sugar, soy sauce, ginger, garlic, and red pepper. Set aside. 2. Mix carrot slices with oil in a medium bowl. season with salt to taste. 3. Arrange the carrots in the Pro-Heat Pan. 4. Install the Accessory Frame in the bottom of the oven, then place the Pro-Heat Pan on top of it. Close the door. 5. Select BROIL. Set the temperature to 400°F and set the time to 30 minutes. Press START/STOP to begin cooking, rotating carrots every 15 minutes for even browning. 6. Brush carrots with the glaze and cook for an additional 3 minutes. 7. Transfer carrots to a serving bowl and drizzle with more glaze. Serve and enjoy!

Serving Suggestions: Garnish with scallion.
Variation Tip: You can use black pepper instead of red pepper.
Nutritional Information per Serving:
Calories: 179 | Fat: 7g|Sat Fat: 1g|Carbohydrates: 29g|Fiber: 3g|Sugar: 23g|Protein: 2g

Tasty Stuffed Poblano Peppers

Prep Time: 10 minutes | Cook Time: 10 minutes | Servings: 4

 **Ingredients:**

4 large poblano peppers
½ cup uncooked brown rice
1½ cups Fresh Grilled Salsa
1 15-ounce can of black beans
1½ cups frozen corn

1 teaspoon cumin
1 teaspoon chili powder
⅛ teaspoon cayenne pepper
Freshly ground black pepper to taste
½ cup cheddar cheese, shredded

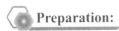 **Preparation:**

1. Cook the rice as directed on its packet. 2. Slice each poblano pepper in half lengthwise and remove their seeds and ribs. 3. Arrange the poblano peppers in the Pro-Heat Pan and shower with cooking oil spray. 4. Install the Accessory Frame in top level of the oven, then place the Pro-Heat Pan on top of it. Close the door. 5. Select BROIL. Set the temperature to 425°F and set the time to 5 minutes. Press START/STOP to begin cooking, tossing them in between. 6. Meanwhile, drain and rinse the black beans. Combine the beans, corn, salsa, a quarter cup of cheese, chili powder, cumin, and cayenne in a large microwave-safe bowl. 7. Season to taste with salt and pepper. Heat the filling in the microwave for about 2 to 3 minutes or until warm, stirring after each 30-second increment. Add the rice and mix well. 8. Fill each pepper half with the filling. Top with the remaining cheese and broil for 2 minutes more or until the cheese melts. 9. Serve and enjoy!

Serving Suggestions: Top with parsley.
Variation Tip: You can also add chopped onion.
Nutritional Information per Serving:
Calories: 543 | Fat: 2g|Sat Fat: 0.6g|Carbohydrates: 45g|Fiber: 12g|Sugar: 15g|Protein: 26g

Cheesy Potato Croquettes

Prep Time: 15 minutes | Cook Time: 23 minutes | Servings: 4

 Ingredients:

2 medium Russet potatoes, peeled and cubed
2 tablespoons all-purpose flour
½ cup Parmesan cheese, grated
1 egg yolk
2 tablespoons chives, minced
A pinch of ground nutmeg

1 pinch Salt
Black pepper, as needed
2 eggs
2 tablespoons vegetable oil
½ cup breadcrumbs

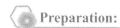 Preparation:

1. In a pan of boiling water, add potatoes and cook for about 15 minutes. 2. Drain the potatoes well and transfer them to a large bowl. 3. Mash the potatoes with a potato masher and set aside to cool completely. 4. Add the flour, egg yolk, chives, Parmesan cheese, salt, nutmeg, and black pepper in the same bowl of mashed potatoes. Whisk until well combined. 5. Make equal-sized small balls from the mixture. 6. Roll each ball into a cylinder shape. 7. In a shallow bowl, crack the eggs and beat well. 8. In another bowl, mix the breadcrumbs and oil. 9. Dip the croquettes in egg mixture and then evenly coat with the breadcrumbs mixture. Place the balls in the Pro-Heat Pan in a single layer. 10. Install the Accessory Frame in top level of the oven. Place the pan in the unit and close the door. 11. Select BROIL. Set the temperature to 400°F and set the time to 8 minutes. Press START/STOP to begin cooking. Enjoy!

Serving Suggestions: Serve with mayonnaise and pink sauce and garnish with cilantro.
Variation Tip: You can use mozzarella cheese or cheddar cheese as a variation.
Nutritional Information per Serving:
Calories: 291| Fat: 14g|Sat Fat: 0.3g|Carbohydrates: 30.3g|Fiber: 6.9g|Sugar: 2.3g|Protein: 11.9g

Hasselback Potatoes with Cheese

Prep Time: 15 minutes | Cook Time: 20 minutes | Servings: 4

 **Ingredients:**

4 medium russet potatoes, scrubbed
4 ounces Parmesan cheese, 2 ounces grated, 2 ounces thinly sliced
4 large cloves garlic, thinly sliced

2 tablespoons olive oil
Kosher salt
Freshly ground black pepper

 Preparation:

1. Place each potato cut between two chopsticks and slice vertically every ⅛ inch, but not to the bottom. 2. Then, remove the ends of each potato. Rinse the potatoes under running water. 3. Place potatoes on a platter and microwave for 5 minutes on high. Microwave the potatoes for another 5 minutes on the other side. 4. Insert garlic and Parmesan slices into slits in the potatoes. 5. Brush olive oil over potatoes and sprinkle with salt and pepper. Top with grated Parmesan cheese. Arrange them in the Roast Rack. 6. Install the Accessory Frame in the bottom of the oven, then place the Pro-Heat Pan on top of it. 7. Place the Roast Rack in the pan and close the door. 8. While holding the smoke box open, use the pellet scoop to pour pellets into the smoke box until filled to the top. Then close the smoke box. 9. Turn dial to select SMOKER, set the temperature to 450°F, and set the time to 10 minutes. Select START/STOP to begin cooking, tossing once in between. 10. Dole out on a plate when roasted and serve topped with mirin mixture. 11. Serve and enjoy!

Serving Suggestions: Serve with ketchup.
Variation Tip: You can use any cheese.
Nutritional Information per Serving:
Calories: 352 | Fat: 15g | Sat Fat: 5g | Carbohydrates: 42g | Fiber: 4g | Sugar: 2g | Protein: 13g

Chapter 3 Snack and Appetizer Recipes

Tasty Baked Hush Puppies

Prep Time: 10 minutes | Cook Time: 10 minutes | Servings: 10

 Ingredients:

1 large egg
½ cup half & half
1 tablespoon white vinegar
1 tablespoon sugar
½ tablespoon onion powder
1 teaspoon sea salt, fine grind

¼ teaspoon chipotle
1 teaspoon baking powder
1 cup cornmeal
1 cup flour all-purpose
½ cup corn frozen or canned, drained
¼ cup white sugar, for coating

 Preparation:

1. Install the Accessory Frame in the bottom level of the unit. Turn left-hand dial to select BAKE. Set the temperature to 400°F and set the time to 10 minutes. Select START/STOP to begin preheating. 2. In a medium bowl, whisk in the egg, half and half, and vinegar. 3. Then stir in the sugar, salt, chipotle, cornmeal, onion powder, and baking powder. 4. Add flour to the mixture and combine well. 5. Fold corn in the batter and mix well. 6. Take one tablespoon full of the batter and shape it into a ball. 7. Place sugar in a shallow dish and roll the balls in the sugar. Then place the hush puppies in one layer in the Pro-Heat Pan and spray with the oil. 8. When unit is preheated and ADD FOOD and PRS STRT is displayed, open the door, place the pan in the unit. Close the door and select START/ STOP to begin cooking. Flip them halfway through the cooking time. 9. When cooking is complete, allow the hush puppies to cool on the cooling rack. Serve and enjoy!

Serving Suggestions: Serve with sour cream and garnish with chopped Parsley and lemon wedges.
Variation Tip: You can add smoked paprika to the mixture.
Nutritional Information per Serving:
Calories: 164 | Fat: 3g | Sat Fat: 1g | Carbohydrates: 30g | Fiber: 2g | Sugar: 7g | Protein: 4g

Homemade Tortilla Chips

Prep Time: 5 minutes | Cook Time: 7 minutes | Servings: 2

 Ingredients:

6 corn tortillas
Salt, as required

Oil, for spraying

 Preparation:

1. Stack tortillas on one another and cut them in triangles. 2. Spray tortilla triangles with oil and season with salt. Place them in the Pro-Heat Pan. 3. Install the Accessory Frame in top level of the oven, then place the Pro-Heat Pan on top of it. Close the door. 4. Select BROIL. Set the temperature to 400°F and set the time to 7 minutes. Press START/STOP to begin cooking. Shake mid-way through the cooking time. 5. Serve and enjoy!

Serving Suggestions: You can serve it with salsa and sour cream.
Variation Tip: You can also garnish with parmesan cheese.
Nutritional Information per Serving:
Calories: 85 | Fat: 1g | Sat Fat: 1g | Carbohydrates: 17g | Fiber: 2g | Sugar: 1g | Protein: 2g

Beef Meatballs

Prep Time: 10 minutes | Cook Time: 10 minutes | Servings: 6

 Ingredients:

1 lb. ground beef
1 ½ tablespoons Worcestershire sauce
¾ teaspoon sea salt
¾ teaspoon basil
¾ teaspoon onion powder

1 large egg
⅓ cup bread crumbs
¼ teaspoon black pepper
¾ teaspoon garlic powder

Preparation:

1. In a mixing bowl, combine the ground beef with all the seasonings and ingredients. Stir to mix well. Shape 2 tbsps of the mixture into a ball. 2. Grease the inside of the Pro-Heat Pan with oil and place the meatballs inside. 3. Install the Accessory Frame in top level of the oven, then place the Pro-Heat Pan on top of it. Close the door. 4. Select BROIL. Set the temperature to 375°F and set the time to 10 minutes. Press START/STOP to begin cooking. Flip the meatballs halfway through the cooking time. 5. The internal temp should be 165°F/75°C. Remove and Serve!

Serving Suggestions: Serve with fresh thyme on top.
Variation Tip: You can add white pepper for taste variation.
Nutritional Information per Serving:
Calories: 253.9 | Fat: 1.1g | Sat Fat: 0.3g | Carbohydrates: 21g | Fiber: 2.6g | Sugar: 0g | Protein: 25g

Crispy Banana Chips

Prep Time: 5 minutes | Cook Time: 10 minutes | Servings: 2

 Ingredients:

4 bananas, barely ripe
2 teaspoons avocado oil

¼ teaspoon kosher salt

Preparation:

1. Cut the bananas into ¼-inch thick slices and place in a bowl. 2. Mix the oil in the banana slices until well coated. Sprinkle with salt. 3. Place a single layer of banana slices in the Pro-Heat Pan. 4. Install the Accessory Frame in top level of the oven, then place the Pro-Heat Pan on top of it. Close the door. 5. Select BROIL. Set the temperature to 350°F and set the time to 10 minutes. Press START/STOP to begin cooking, flipping halfway through, until bananas are lightly brown and crispy. 6. Remove from the oven and let cool on a cooling rack. 7. Repeat with remaining bananas.

Serving Suggestions: Serve with ketchup.
Variation Tip: Add in some paprika powder for taste variation.
Nutritional Information per Serving:
Calories: 216 | Fat: 1.4g | Sat Fat: 0.4g | Carbohydrates: 54.2g | Fiber: 6.3g | Sugar: 28.9g | Protein: 2.6g

Rice Bites with Cheese

Prep Time: 15 minutes | Cook Time: 10 minutes | Servings: 4

 **Ingredients:**

3 cups cooked risotto

⅓ cup Parmesan cheese, grated

1 egg, beaten

3 ounces mozzarella cheese, cubed

¾ cup breadcrumbs

 Preparation:

1. In a bowl, mix together the risotto, egg and Parmesan cheese. 2. Make 20 equal-sized balls from the mixture. 3. Place a mozzarella cube in the center of each ball, and smooth the risotto mixture to cover the mozzarella. 4. Coat the balls evenly with breadcrumbs. Then place the balls in a single layer in the Pro-Heat Pan. Close the door. 5. Select BROIL. Set the temperature to 390°F and set the time to 10 minutes. Press START/STOP to begin cooking. Cook until they are golden brown. 6. Serve!

Serving Suggestions: Serve it with your favorite dip and garnish with chives.

Variation Tip: You can add any other cheese.

Nutritional Information per Serving:

Calories: 279 | Fat: 7.3g | Sat Fat: 7g | Carbohydrates: 50.7g | Fiber: 1.2g | Sugar: 0.6g | Protein: 9.4g

Homemade Garlic Knots

Prep Time: 10 minutes | Cook Time: 16 minutes | Servings: 8

 Ingredients:

1-pound raw pizza dough

2 bulbs of whole raw garlic

2 tablespoons olive oil

6 tablespoons salted butter melted, divided into recipe

1 teaspoon Italian seasoning

1 teaspoon garlic powder

½ teaspoon fine grind sea salt

1 teaspoon dried parsley

 Preparation:

1. In a pan, sauté the olive oil and garlic cloves for 6 minutes. 2. When garlic is caramelized, transfer it to a bowl and strain excessive oil. Set it aside. 3. In a separate bowl, add melted butter, sea salt, garlic powder and Italian seasoning. Mash the roasted garlic and add in the butter mixture. 4. Divide the pizza dough into 16 equal pieces. 5. Roll the ball into a 6" long rope and tie the rope into a knot. 6. Dip each knot into the garlic butter mixture and arrange them in the Pro-Heat Pan about 1-inch apart. 7. Install the Accessory Frame in the bottom level of the unit. Turn left-hand dial to select BAKE. Set the temperature to 400°F and set the time to 10 minutes. Select START/STOP to begin preheating. 8. When unit is preheated and ADD FOOD and PRS STRT is displayed, open the door, place the pan in the unit. Close the door and select START/ STOP to begin cooking. 9. Once all the garlic knots are done, place them on a cooling rack and brush them with the remaining garlic butter.

Serving Suggestions: Serve it with parsley and parmesan cheese.

Variation Tip: You can also top it with grated mozzarella cheese.

Nutritional Information per Serving:

Calories: 203| Fat: 10g|Sat Fat: 6g|Carbohydrates: 25g|Fiber: 2g|Sugar: 0.1g|Protein: 4g

Lime Honey Pineapple

Prep Time: 5 minutes | Cook Time: 6 minutes | Servings: 6

 **Ingredients:**

1 fresh pineapple
3 tablespoons brown sugar
1 tablespoon lime juice
1 tablespoon olive oil

1 tablespoon honey
1½ teaspoons chili powder
Dash salt

 **Preparation:**

1. Remove any eyeballs from the pineapple and peel it. Remove the core and cut lengthwise into six wedges. 2. Mix the remaining ingredients to make the glaze. Brush the pineapple with half of the glaze. 3. Arrange them in the Pro-Heat Pan and shower with olive oil. 4. Install the Accessory Frame in the bottom of the oven, then place the Pro-Heat Pan on top of it. 5. While holding the smoke box open, use the pellet scoop to pour pellets into the smoke box until filled to the top. Then close the smoke box. 6. Turn dial to select SMOKER, set the temperature to 450°F, and set the time to 6 minutes. Select START/STOP to begin cooking, turning them occasionally. 7. Serve and enjoy!

Serving Suggestions: Serve with steak.
Variation Tip: You can use agave nectar instead of honey.
Nutritional Information per Serving:
Calories: 97 | Fat: 2g | Sat Fat: 0g | Carbohydrates: 50g | Fiber: 1g | Sugar: 13g | Protein: 1g

Mozzarella Crisp Sticks

Prep Time: 15 minutes | Cook Time: 12 minutes | Servings: 4

 Ingredients:

¼ cup white flour
2 eggs
3 tablespoons nonfat milk

1 cup plain breadcrumbs
1-pound Mozzarella cheese block, cut into 3x½-inch sticks

 **Preparation:**

1. Place the flour in a shallow bowl. 2. In a second bowl, whisk the eggs and milk. 3. Add the breadcrumbs to a separate shallow bowl and set aside. 4. Coat the Mozzarella sticks in the flour; dip into the egg mixture, and finally, coat evenly with the breadcrumbs. 5. Arrange the Mozzarella sticks onto a baking sheet and freeze for about 1 to 2 hours. Then place them in the Pro-Heat Pan in a single layer. 6. Install the Accessory Frame in top level of the oven, then place the Pro-Heat Pan on top of it. Close the door. 7. Select BROIL. Set the temperature to 400°F and set the time to 12 minutes. Press START/STOP to begin cooking. 8. You can do this in two batches. 9. Enjoy!

Serving Suggestions: Serve with your favorite dipping sauce.
Variation Tip: You can add flavored seasoning to the breadcrumbs to give them some flavor variation.
Nutritional Information per Serving:
Calories: 191| Fat: 5g|Sat Fat: 5g|Carbohydrates: 26.4g|Fiber: 5.5g|Sugar: 2.4g|Protein: 9.6g

Easy Broiled Pickles

Prep Time: 15 minutes | Cook Time: 5 minutes | Servings: 10

 **Ingredients:**

3 whole dill pickles
¼ cup all-purpose flour
Wet Batter:
1 large egg
1 tablespoon mustard
Breadcrumb Coating:
1 cup breadcrumbs
½ teaspoon garlic powder
½ teaspoon onion powder

1 tablespoon avocado oil, for spraying

½ cup beer or water
¾ cup all-purpose flour

½ teaspoon cumin
½ teaspoon smoked paprika
¼ teaspoon fine grind sea salt

 **Preparation:**

1. Cut the pickles into ¼-½" slices. Place them in a bowl and toss with all-purpose flour. 2. Combine all the wet batter ingredients in a second bowl to make a lump-free batter. 3. In a third bowl, combine the bread crumbs and seasonings to make the coating. 4. Coat each pickle with wet batter and dry coating, respectively. 5. Spray the inside of the Pro-Heat Pan with the avocado spray. Place the coated pickles in the pan in a single layer. 6. Install the Accessory Frame in top level of the oven, then place the Pro-Heat Pan on top of it. Close the door. 7. Select BROIL. Set the temperature to 400°F and set the time to 5 minutes. Press START/STOP to begin cooking. Cook until they are golden brown. 8. Once they are done, place them on the cooling rack and repeat if you have multiple batches.

Serving Suggestions: Serve with your favorite dipping sauce.
Variation Tip: You can use olive oil instead of avocado oil.
Nutritional Information per Serving:
Calories: 115 Fat: 3g|Sat Fat: 1g|Carbohydrates: 18g|Fiber: 1g|Sugar: 1g|Protein: 4g

Roasted Crunchy Chickpeas

Prep Time: 5 minutes | Cook Time: 10 minutes | Servings: 4

 **Ingredients:**

3 cups chickpeas, cooked
1 tablespoon avocado oil
1 teaspoon sea salt

1 teaspoon cumin
½ teaspoon garlic powder
½ teaspoon onion powder

 **Preparation:**

1. Drain the chickpeas and place them on the paper towel to dry excess moisture. 2. Add oil to the chickpeas and season with salt and other spices. Place chickpeas in the Pro-Heat Pan. 3. Install the Accessory Frame in top level of the oven, then place the Pro-Heat Pan on top of it. Close the door. 4. Select BROIL. Set the temperature to 425°F and set the time to 10 minutes. Press START/STOP to begin cooking, tossing them in between. 5. Remove them from the oven and lay them on a cooling rack to keep them crisp. 6. Serve and Enjoy!

Serving Suggestions: Serve with Lime Wedges
Variation Tip: You can use any other seasoning of your choice, e.g., BBQ seasoning, Lime and herb seasoning, etc.
Nutritional Information per Serving:
Calories: 142| Fat: 6g|Sat Fat: 1g|Carbohydrates: 17g|Fiber: 6g|Sugar: 1g|Protein: 6g

Chapter 4 Poultry Recipes

Roasted Herb Whole Chicken

Prep Time: 10 minutes | Cook Time: 30 minutes | Servings: 7

 Ingredients:

2 tablespoons butter

3 garlic cloves, minced

1 teaspoon lemon zest, grated

1 teaspoon dried thyme, crushed

1 teaspoon dried oregano, crushed

1 teaspoon dried rosemary, crushed

1 teaspoon smoked paprika

Salt to taste

Pepper to taste

2 tablespoons lemon juice

2 tablespoons sesame oil

1 whole chicken

 Preparation:

1. Mix together the garlic, herbs, lemon zest and spices in a bowl. 2. Rub the chicken evenly with the herb mixture. 3. Drizzle some oil and lemon juice on the chicken. Set aside overnight. 4. Install the Accessory Frame in the bottom of the oven, then place the Pro-Heat Pan on top of it. 5. Place the chicken in the Roast Rack, and then place rack in the Pro-Heat Pan. Close the door. 6. While holding the smoke box open, use the pellet scoop to pour pellets into the smoke box until filled to the top. Then close the smoke box. 7. Turn dial to select SMOKER, set the temperature to 500°F, and set the time to 30 minutes. Select START/STOP to begin cooking, flipping the side after 15 minutes. 8. Serve and enjoy.

Serving Suggestions: Serve with mayo dip.

Variation Tip: You can skip cayenne pepper

Nutritional Information per Serving:

Calories: 860 | Fat: 50g | Sat Fat: 24g | Carbohydrates: 1.3g | Fiber: 2g | Sugar: 0.2g | Protein: 71.1g

Spicy Wings with Sauce

Prep Time: 10 minutes | Cook Time: 30 minutes | Servings: 4

 Ingredients:

4 pounds chicken wings

2 tablespoons Goya Adobo Seasoning

2 cups Buffalo Sauce

Cooking Spray

Preparation:

1. In a bowl, add all ingredients except for chicken wings. Stir to mix well. 2. Add in the chicken wings and toss to coat well. Let the wings sit for 20 minutes. 3. Install the Accessory Frame in top level of the oven. Place the marinated chicken in the Pro-Heat Pan and place the pan in the unit. Close the door. 4. Select BROIL. Set the temperature to 400°F and set the time to 30 minutes. Press START/STOP to begin cooking. 5. Serve warm and enjoy.

Serving Suggestions: Serve with hot sauce on top.

Variation Tip: You can add crushed chili flakes to spice it more up.

Nutritional Information per Serving:

Calories: 557|Fat: 39g|Sat Fat: 11g|Carbohydrates: 3g|Fiber: 1g|Sugar: 1g|Protein: 46g

Simple Sweet & Sour Turkey Wings

Prep Time: 15 minutes | Cook Time: 30 minutes | Servings: 6

 Ingredients:

6 turkey wings
8 cups water
¼ cup red wine vinegar
2 tablespoons dark soy sauce
1½ tablespoons light brown sugar

¾ teaspoon dried thyme
1 teaspoon Tabasco sauce
3 garlic cloves, finely chopped
2 scallions, finely chopped

 Preparation:

1. Add turkey wings to a pot of water and bring to a boil. 2. Cover and boil for about 15 minutes. 3. Remove the pot of turkey from heat and set aside. 4. Remove the wings from pot of water and place onto the Roast Rack. 5. With your hands, gently press down each wing.
6. Install the Accessory Frame in the bottom of the oven, then place the Pro-Heat Pan on top of it. Then place the rack with turkey wings onto the pan. Close the door. 7. While holding the smoke box open, use the pellet scoop to pour pellets into the smoke box until filled to the top. Then close the smoke box. 8. Turn dial to select SMOKER, set the temperature to 450°F, and set the time to 30 minutes. Select START/STOP to begin cooking. 9. Meanwhile, mix together all the remaining ingredients in a bowl. After 12 minutes of cooking, flip the wings and brush with the sauce evenly. 10. After 24 minutes of cooking, flip the wings and brush with the sauce again. 11. When cook time is complete, transfer the wings onto a platter. 12. Coat the wings with any remaining sauce and serve immediately.

Serving Suggestions: Serve with a garnishing of scallion greens.
Variation Tip: Red wine vinegar can be replaced with balsamic vinegar too.
Nutritional Information per Serving:
Calories: 6118 | Fat: 37.8g | Sat Fat: 0g | Carbohydrates: 3.3g | Fiber: 0.2g | Sugar: 2.4g | Protein: 62.7g

Chicken with Teriyaki Sauce

Prep Time: 10 minutes | Cook Time: 10 minutes | Servings: 6

 Ingredients:

2 chicken thighs, cubed

¾ cup Teriyaki Sauce

Preparation:

1. Place chicken in the Pro-Heat Pan and brush with teriyaki sauce. 2. Install the Accessory Frame in top level of the oven, then place the Pro-Heat Pan on top of it. Close the door. 3. Select BROIL. Set the temperature to 425°F and set the time to 10 minutes. Press START/STOP to begin cooking. Flip the side after half time, brush with teriyaki sauce the other side too. 4. When cook time is complete, sprinkle sesame seeds on it. 5. Serve with anything you like and enjoy!

Serving Suggestions: Serve with a bowl of white rice.
Variation Tip: You can add some crushed chili flakes for some spiced up taste.
Nutritional Information per Serving:
Calories: 282|Fat: 19g|Sat Fat: 3g|Carbohydrates: 6g|Fiber: 1g|Sugar: 3g|Protein: 21g

Homemade Turkey Burgers

Prep Time: 15 minutes | Cook Time: 10 minutes | Servings: 4

Ingredients:

1-pound ground turkey
1 large egg, lightly beaten
½ cup seasoned breadcrumbs

Salt and ground black pepper, as required
1 tablespoon olive oil

Preparation:

1. In a large bowl, mix together the ground turkey, breadcrumbs, egg, salt, and black pepper. 2. Make 4 (½-inch-thick) patties from the mixture. 3. Using your thumb, press a shallow indentation in the center of each patty. 4. Brush both sides of each patty with oil. 5. Arrange the patties in the lightly greased Pro-Heat Pan. 6. Install the Accessory Frame in the bottom of the oven, then place the Pro-Heat Pan on top of it. Close the door. 7. While holding the smoke box open, use the pellet scoop to pour pellets into the smoke box until filled to the top. Then close the smoke box. 8. Turn dial to select SMOKER, set the temperature to 450°F, and set the time to 10 minutes. Select START/STOP to begin cooking. Flip the patties halfway through the cooking time. 9. When the cooking time is completed, remove to a platter and serve hot.

Serving Suggestions: Serve alongside the buttered potatoes.
Variation Tip: You can use breadcrumbs of your choice.
Nutritional Information per Serving:
Calories: 265 | Fat: 14.6g | Sat Fat: 2.9g | Carbohydrates: 8.6g | Fiber: 0.5g | Sugar: 0.1g | Protein: 27.4g

Quick Chipotle Turkey Burger

Prep Time: 15 minutes | Cook Time: 10 minutes | Servings: 4

Ingredients:

1 pound extra lean ground turkey
2-2¼ tablespoons chipotle chile in adobo sauce, pureed
1 garlic clove, minced

1 tablespoon red chili powder
Salt and ground black pepper, as required

Preparation:

1. In a bowl, combine ground turkey and remaining ingredients and stir to mix well. 2. Refrigerate for about 6-8 hours. 3. Make 4 equal-sized patties from the mixture. 4. Place the patties in the lightly greased Pro-Heat Pan. With your thumb, make a slight dent in the center of each patty. 5. Install the Accessory Frame in the bottom of the oven, then place the Pro-Heat Pan on top of it. Close the door. 6. While holding the smoke box open, use the pellet scoop to pour pellets into the smoke box until filled to the top. Then close the smoke box. 7. Turn dial to select SMOKER, set the temperature to 450°F, and set the time to 10 minutes. Select START/STOP to begin cooking. Flip the patties halfway through the cooking time. 8. When the cooking time is up, remove the patties to a platter and serve hot.

Serving Suggestions: Serve these patties in your favorite burger.
Variation Tip: You can skip the red chili powder.
Nutritional Information per Serving:
Calories: 180 | Fat: 8.4g | Sat Fat: 2.6g | Carbohydrates: 1.5g | Fiber: 0.7g | Sugar: 0.3g | Protein: 21.6g

Grilled Turkey & Apple Burgers

Prep Time: 15 minutes | Cook Time: 12 minutes | Servings: 2

 **Ingredients:**

6 ounces lean ground turkey
½ of small apple, peeled, cored and grated
2 tablespoons red onion, minced
1 small garlic clove, minced
½ tablespoon fresh ginger, minced

1 tablespoon fresh cilantro, chopped
¼ teaspoon ground cumin
Salt and ground black pepper, as required
Non-stick cooking spray

Preparation:

1. In a bowl, add all the ingredients and mix until well combined. 2. Shape the mixture into 2 patties. 3. Spray each patty with cooking spray and arrange them in the lightly greased Pro-Heat Pan. 4. Install the Accessory Frame in the bottom of the oven, then place the Pro-Heat Pan on top of it. Close the door. 5. While holding the smoke box open, use the pellet scoop to pour pellets into the smoke box until filled to the top. Then close the smoke box. 6. Turn dial to select SMOKER, set the temperature to 450°F, and set the time to 12 minutes. Select START/STOP to begin cooking. Flip the patties halfway through the cooking time. 7. When cooking time is up, remove the patties to a platter and serve hot .

Serving Suggestions: Serve alongside the spinach and tomato salad.
Variation Tip: Don't use tart apple.
Nutritional Information per Serving:
Calories: 167 | Fat: 6.5g | Sat Fat: 1.5g | Carbohydrates: 10.6g | Fiber: 2.4g | Sugar: 6.4g | Protein: 18g

Broiled Chicken Skewers

Prep Time: 40 minutes | Cook Time: 6 minutes | Servings: 6

 **Ingredients:**

1½ lbs. chicken breast boneless, cubed
½ cup coconut milk
2 cloves garlic minced
2 teaspoons ginger
2 teaspoons turmeric

1 teaspoon sea salt fine grind
1 tablespoon lemongrass paste
1 tablespoon chili garlic sauce
2 teaspoons lemon juice

Preparation:

1. In a bowl, add ingredients except for chicken. Stir to mix well. 2. Add in the chicken and toss until well coated. Marinate the chicken with sauce mixture and let sit for 30 minutes. 3. Afterwards, set the chicken pieces on wooden skewers. 4. Arrange them in the Roast Rack. 5. Install the Accessory Frame in top level of the oven, then place the Pro-Heat Pan on top of it. Place the Roast Rack in the pan. Close the door. 6. Select BROIL. Set the temperature to 425°F and set the time to 6 minutes. Press START/STOP to begin cooking, flipping the sides after 3 minutes.

Serving Suggestions: Serve with chopped cilantro on top.
Variation Tip: Almond oil can also be used instead of coconut oil.
Nutritional Information per Serving:
Calories: 177| Fat: 7g|Sat Fat: 4g|Carbohydrates: 3g|Fiber: 1g|Sugar: 1g|Protein: 25g

Tasty Turkey Meatballs Kabobs

Prep Time: 15 minutes | Cook Time: 14 minutes | Servings: 4

 Ingredients:

1 yellow onion, chopped roughly
½ cup lemongrass, chopped roughly
2 garlic cloves, chopped roughly
1½ pounds lean ground turkey
1 teaspoon sesame oil

½ tablespoons low-sodium soy sauce
1 tablespoon arrowroot starch
⅛ teaspoon powdered stevia
Salt and ground black pepper, as required

 Preparation:

1. Combine the onion, lemongrass, and garlic in a food processor and pulse until finely chopped. 2. Transfer the onion mixture to a large bowl. 3. Add the remaining ingredients and stir until well combined. 4. Make 12 equal-sized balls from meat mixture. 5. Thread the balls onto the presoaked wooden skewers. 6. Then arrange the Meatballs Kabobs in the Roast Rack. 7. Install the Accessory Frame in the bottom of the oven, then place the Pro-Heat Pan on top of it. Place the Roast Rack in the pan. Close the door. 8. While holding the smoke box open, use the pellet scoop to pour pellets into the smoke box until filled to the top. Then close the smoke box. 9. Turn dial to select SMOKER, set the temperature to 450°F, and set the time to 14 minutes. Select START/STOP to begin cooking. Flip the skewers halfway through the cooking time. 10. When cooking time is up, remove the Meatballs Kabobs to a platter and serve hot.

Serving Suggestions: Serve alongside the tzatziki sauce.
Variation Tip: Make sure to use lean ground turkey.
Nutritional Information per Serving:
Calories: 276 | Fat: 13.4g | Sat Fat: 4g | Carbohydrates: 5.6g | Fiber: 0.6g | Sugar: 1.3g | Protein: 34.2g

Butter Crispy Chicken Tenders

Prep Time: 10 minutes | Cook Time: 10 minutes | Servings: 4

 Ingredients:

2 tablespoons butter
4 chicken breasts, cut into tenders
1 egg white
⅛ cup flour

½ cup panko bread crumbs
Salt, to taste
Pepper, to taste

 Preparation:

1. Place the chicken tenders in a bowl and season with melted butter, salt and black pepper. 2. Coat chicken tenders with flour, dip in egg whites and then dredge with bread crumbs. 3. Place the chicken wings in the Pro-Heat Pan. 4. Install the Accessory Frame in the bottom of the oven, then place the Pro-Heat Pan on top of it. Close the door. 5. Select BROIL. Set the temperature to 400°F and set the time to 10 minutes. Press START/STOP to begin cooking. 6. Serve warm.

Serving Suggestions: Serve with garlic mayo.
Variation Tip: You can add grated parmesan too.
Nutritional Information per Serving:
Calories: 250|Fat: 9.3g|Sat Fat: 3.8g|Carbohydrates: 12.8g|Fiber: 0.7g|Sugar: 0.9g|Protein: 26.9g

Thyme Grilled Duck Breasts

Prep Time: 10 minutes | Cook Time: 16 minutes | Servings: 2

 **Ingredients:**

2 shallots, sliced thinly
1 tablespoon fresh ginger, minced
2 tablespoons fresh thyme, chopped

Salt and ground black pepper, as required
2 duck breasts

 **Preparation:**

1. Add the shallots, ginger, salt, thyme, and black pepper to a large bowl, and mix well. 2. Add in the duck breasts and toss to coat evenly. 3. Marinate in the refrigerator for about 2–12 hours.
4. Install the Accessory Frame in top level of the oven, then place the Pro-Heat Pan on top of it. Place the Roast Rack in the pan. 5. Place the marinated duck breasts onto the Roast Rack and close the door. 6. While holding the smoke box open, use the pellet scoop to pour pellets into the smoke box until filled to the top. Then close the smoke box. 7. Turn dial to select SMOKER, set the temperature to 450°F, and set the time to 16 minutes. Select START/STOP to begin cooking. Flip the duck breasts halfway through the cooking time. 8. When the cooking time is completed, remove to a platter and serve hot.

Serving Suggestions: Serve alongside the steamed broccoli.
Variation Tip: Try to use Pekin duck breast.
Nutritional Information per Serving:
Calories: 337 | Fat: 10.1g | Sat Fat: 0g | Carbohydrates: 3.4g | Fiber: 0g | Sugar: 0.8g | Protein: 55.5g

Air Crisp Chicken Wings

Prep Time: 10 minutes | Cook Time: 15 minutes | Servings: 6

 Ingredients:

2 lbs. chicken wings
2 tablespoons smoked paprika
3 teaspoons cayenne pepper
2 teaspoons chili powder
2 teaspoons honey

1 tablespoon black pepper
1½ teaspoons garlic powder
2 teaspoons onion powder
1½ teaspoons Italian seasoning
1½ teaspoons dried thyme

Preparation:

1. Combine all ingredients in a bowl except for chicken wings. Mix well. 2. Marinade chicken wings with the honey sauce mixture for 20 minutes. 3. Then place the marinated chicken wings in the Pro-Heat Pan. 4. Install the Accessory Frame in the bottom of the oven, then place the Pro-Heat Pan on top of it. Close the door. 5. Select BROIL. Set the temperature to 400°F and set the time to 15 minutes. Press START/STOP to begin cooking. 6. Serve warm and enjoy.

Serving Suggestions: Serve with cilantro on top.
Variation Tip: Cayenne pepper can be skipped.
Nutritional Information per Serving:
Calories: 211|Fat: 15g|Sat Fat: 4g|Carbohydrates: 5.2g|Fiber: 2g|Sugar: 1.2g|Protein: 16g

Garlic Chicken Breasts with Sauce

Prep Time: 15 minutes | Cook Time: 23 minutes | Servings: 4

 **Ingredients:**

4 chicken breasts

⅓ cup olive oil

3 tablespoons soy sauce

1 tablespoon Worcestershire sauce

2 tablespoons balsamic vinegar

¼ cup brown sugar

3 teaspoons garlic, minced

Salt and ground black pepper, as required

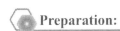 **Preparation:**

1. Use a fork to poke each chicken breast. 2. In a large bowl, blend together oil, soy sauce, vinegar, Worcestershire sauce, garlic, brown sugar, salt and black pepper to make the marinade. 3. In a small bowl, place ¼ cup of the marinade and reserve in the refrigerator. 4. In the bowl of remaining marinade, add the chicken breasts and stir until well coated. 5. Set aside for about 20 minutes. 6. Install the Accessory Frame in top level of the oven, then place the Pro-Heat Pan on top of it. Place the Roast Rack in the pan. 7. Transfer the marinated chicken breasts onto the Roast Rack. Close the door. 8. While holding the smoke box open, use the pellet scoop to pour pellets into the smoke box until filled to the top. Then close the smoke box. 9. Turn dial to select SMOKER, set the temperature to 450°F, and set the time to 23 minutes. Select START/STOP to begin cooking. 10. After 15 minutes of cooking, flip the chicken breasts and brush with half of the reserved marinade. 11. After 20 minutes of cooking, flip the chicken breasts again and brush with the remaining reserved marinade. 12. Once done, serve hot.

Serving Suggestions: Serve with garnishing of lemon slices.

Variation Tip: Try to use low-sodium soy sauce.

Nutritional Information per Serving:

Calories: 345 | Fat: 18.7g | Sat Fat: 2.4g | Carbohydrates: 11.3g | Fiber: 0.1g | Sugar: 9.8g | Protein: 33.8g

Cream Cheese Bacon and Chicken

Prep Time: 10 minutes | Cook Time: 30 minutes | Servings: 6

 Ingredients:

6 chicken breasts

½ cup water

2 cup cream cheese

7 slices bacon, cooked and chopped

1 cup shredded cheese

Half package of ranch dry mix

 Preparation:

1. In a skillet over medium heat, add in water, cream cheese, ranch and bring to a simmer. 2. Once the ranch mixture is thick, remove from heat and coat chicken with it really well. 3. Place the chicken in Pro-Heat Pan. Drizzle the chicken with the ranch sauce and top with bacon. 4. Install the Accessory Frame in top level of the oven, then place the Pro-Heat Pan on top of it. Close the door. 5. Select BROIL. Set the temperature to 500°F and set the time to 25 minutes. Press START/STOP to begin cooking. 6. Serve warm and enjoy!

Serving Suggestions: Serve with ranch sauce.

Variation Tip: You can add white pepper for taste variation.

Nutritional Information per Serving:

Calories: 594|Fat: 45.3g|Sat Fat: 24g|Carbohydrates: 2.8g|Fiber: 0g|Sugar: 0.3g|Protein: 42.5g

Simple Crispy Chicken Sausages

Prep Time: 5 minutes | Cook Time: 7 minutes | Servings: 6

 **Ingredients:**

12 chicken sausages

Preparation:

1. Place the sausages in the Pro-Heat Pan. 2. Install the Accessory Frame in top level of the oven, then place the Pro-Heat Pan on top of it. Close the door. 3. Select BROIL. Set the temperature to 400°F and set the time to 7 minutes. Press START/STOP to begin cooking, flipping each side after half time. 4. Once done, serve with garlic mayo and enjoy!

Serving Suggestions: Serve with garlic mayo sauce.
Variation Tip: You can use chicken cheese sausages too.
Nutritional Information per Serving:
Calories: 122|Fat: 11g|Sat Fat: 4g|Carbohydrates: 0g|Fiber: 0g|Sugar: 0g|Protein: 6g

Greek Chicken Breast

Prep Time: 20 minutes | Cook Time: 15 minutes | Servings: 4

 Ingredients:

For chicken:
4 chicken breasts
¼ cup extra-virgin olive oil
2 teaspoons dried oregano
For sauce:
½ cup finely grated cucumber
1 cup of Greek yogurt

1 teaspoon garlic powder
1 tablespoon lemon juice

2 teaspoons apple cider vinegar
1 tablespoon of garlic powder

Preparation:

1. In a bowl, mix together the olive oil, garlic powder, oregano and lemon juice. Add in chicken and toss to coat well. Marinade for 10 minutes. 2. Install the Accessory Frame in top level of the oven, then place the Pro-Heat Pan on top of it. Place the Roast Rack in the pan. 3. Arrange the marinated chicken on the Roast Rack and close the door. 4. While holding the smoke box open, use the pellet scoop to pour pellets into the smoke box until filled to the top. Then close the smoke box. 5. Turn dial to select SMOKER, set the temperature to 500°F, and set the time to 15 minutes. Select START/STOP to begin cooking. Flip halfway through the cooking time. 6. Meanwhile, combine all of the sauce ingredients in another bowl. Mix well. 7. Once chicken is cooked, drizzle sauce over it and serve with rice.

Serving Suggestions: Serve with green onions on top.
Variation Tip: You can use any yogurt instead of Greek yogurt.
Nutritional Information per Serving:
Calories: 521 | Fat: 20g | Sat Fat: 4g | Carbohydrates: 26g | Fiber: 2g | Sugar: 18g | Protein: 59g

Yummy Chicken Nuggets

Prep Time: 10 minutes | Cook Time: 10 minutes | Servings: 4

 Ingredients:

½ of zucchini, roughly chopped
½ of carrot, roughly chopped
14 ounces chicken breast, cut into chunks
½ tablespoon mustard powder
1 tablespoon garlic powder
1 tablespoon onion powder

Salt to taste
Pepper to taste
1 cup all-purpose flour
2 tablespoons milk
1 egg
1 cup panko breadcrumbs

 Preparation:

1. In a blender, add the carrot, zucchini, water and blend until finely chopped. 2. Add the chicken, garlic powder, onion powder, mustard powder, salt, and black pepper and blend smoothly. 3. Place flour in a shallow bowl. 4. In another bowl, whisk the egg and milk. 5. Place the breadcrumbs in a third bowl. 6. Roll the nuggets in the flour, then dip into egg mixture and then coat with the breadcrumbs. Set aside for 10 minutes. 7. Place the coated nuggets in the Pro-Heat Pan. 8. Install the Accessory Frame in the bottom of the oven, then place the Pro-Heat Pan on top of it. Close the door. 9. Select BROIL. Set the temperature to 400°F and set the time to 10 minutes. Press START/STOP to begin cooking. Flip halfway through the cooking time. 10. Serve warm and enjoy.

Serving Suggestions: Serve with ketchup on top.
Variation Tip: You can add dried basil leaves.
Nutritional Information per Serving:
Calories: 430|Fat: 7g|Sat Fat: 3g|Carbohydrates: 48.7g|Fiber: 4g|Sugar: 4.2g|Protein: 41.6g

Popcorn Spicy Chicken

Prep Time: 10 minutes | Cook Time: 10 minutes | Servings: 6

 Ingredients:

2 chicken breasts boneless, cut into tenders
1 cup Panko bread crumbs
1 cup all-purpose flour
1 teaspoon chili flakes or more if you want it spicy
2 teaspoons oregano

2 teaspoons onion powder
2 teaspoons garlic powder
2 teaspoons pepper
2 teaspoons salt
1 egg

Preparation:

1. In a bowl, whisk in the egg. 2. Place bread crumbs in another bowl. 3. In a third bowl, combine the flour and remaining spices. 4. Roll the chicken tenders in the flour mix, then dip in the egg and finally coat in the bread crumbs. 5. Arrange the chicken tenders in the Pro-Heat Pan. 6. Install the Accessory Frame in top level of the oven, then place the Pro-Heat Pan on top of it. Close the door. 7. Select BROIL. Set the temperature to 400°F and set the time to 10 minutes. Press START/STOP to begin cooking. 8. Serve with garlic mayo sauce and enjoy!

Serving Suggestions: Serve with BBQ or Peri Peri sauce.
Variation Tip: You can add some parmesan cheese.
Nutritional Information per Serving:
Calories: 253|Fat: 4g|Sat Fat: 1g|Carbohydrates: 31g|Fiber: 2g|Sugar: 1g|Protein: 22g

Roasted Spicy Chicken

Prep Time: 10 minutes | Cook Time: 30 minutes | Servings: 6

 Ingredients:

2 teaspoons dried thyme
2 teaspoons paprika
1 teaspoon cayenne pepper
1 teaspoon onion powder
1 teaspoon garlic powder
Zest of 1 lemon

1 tbsp lemon juice
Salt, to taste
Pepper, to taste
3 tablespoons oil
1 whole chicken

 Preparation:

1. In a bowl, mix the lemon zest, garlic, herbs and spices. 2. Rub the chicken with the herb mixture. 3. Drizzle some oil and lemon juice on the chicken. Set aside overnight. 4. Place the chicken on the Roast Rack. 5. Install the Accessory Frame in top level of the oven, then place the Pro-Heat Pan on top of it. Place the Roast Rack in the pan and close the door. 6. Select BROIL. Set the temperature to 425°F and set the time to 30 minutes. Press START/STOP to begin cooking, flipping the side after 15 minutes. 7. Serve and enjoy.

Serving Suggestions: Serve with veggies.
Variation Tip: You can add ground white pepper for enhancing the taste.
Nutritional Information per Serving:
Calories: 871|Fat: 60g|Sat Fat: 24g|Carbohydrates: 1.7g|Fiber: 2g|Sugar: 0.4g|Protein: 70.6g

Baked Chicken Legs

Prep Time: 10 minutes | Cook Time: 25 minutes | Servings: 3

 **Ingredients:**

3 chicken legs
1 cup buttermilk
2 cups white flour
1 teaspoon garlic powder
1 teaspoon onion powder

1 teaspoon ground cumin
1 teaspoon paprika
Salt to taste
Pepper to taste
1 tablespoon olive oil

 Preparation:

1. In a bowl, combine the chicken legs and buttermilk. 2. Leave it in the refrigerator for about 2 hours. 3. In another bowl, mix together the flour, olive oil, and spices. 4. Remove the chicken from buttermilk and coat with the flour mixture. 5. Repeat this twice with each chicken leg. Season with salt and pepper. Place the chicken legs in the Pro-Heat Pan. 6. Install the Accessory Frame in the bottom level of the unit. Turn left-hand dial to select BAKE. Set the temperature to 400°F and set the time to 25 minutes. Select START/STOP to begin preheating. 7. When unit is preheated and ADD FOOD and PRS STRT is displayed, open the door, place the pan in the unit. Close the door and select START/ STOP to begin cooking, flipping the side after half time. 8. Serve hot.

Serving Suggestions: Serve with baked potatoes.
Variation Tip: You can skip ground cumin.
Nutritional Information per Serving:
Calories: 607|Fat: 22.5g|Sat Fat: 1.3g|Carbohydrates: 71.6g|Fiber: 2.7g|Sugar: 4.7g|Protein: 28.8g

Cheesy Garlic Crusted Chicken

Prep Time: 10 minutes | Cook Time: 20 minutes | Servings: 1

 Ingredients:

2 potatoes, cubed and boiled

1 chicken breast

1 stick butter, melted

1 cup panko bread crumbs

1 egg

1 tablespoon Italian seasonings

½ cup Parm cheese, shredded

1 tablespoons garlic powder

½ tablespoon salt

½ tablespoon pepper

 Preparation:

1. In a bowl, mix together the butter, garlic powder, and seasoning. Pour this mixture over the potatoes. 2. Combine the breadcrumbs and cheese in another bowl. 3. Whisk the egg in a third bowl. 4. Dip the chicken breast in the egg and dredge in the panko mix. Place the chicken and potatoes in the Pro-Heat Pan. 5. Install the Accessory Frame in the bottom of the oven, then place the Pro-Heat Pan on top of it. Close the door. 6. Select BROIL. Set the temperature to 400°F and set the time to 20 minutes. Press START/STOP to begin cooking, flipping the side after half time. 7. Serve warm and enjoy!

Serving Suggestions: Serve with potatoes.

Variation Tip: You can add crushed chili flakes.

Nutritional Information per Serving:

Calories: 1802|Fat: 109.4g|Sat Fat: 61.6g|Carbohydrates: 154.8g|Fiber: 16.8g|Sugar: 15.3g|Protein: 53.8g

French Chicken with Onion

Prep Time: 10 minutes | Cook Time: 15 minutes | Servings: 4

 Ingredients:

2 tablespoons olive oil

2 tablespoons butter

2 large chicken breasts

1 teaspoon sea salt fine grind

1 teaspoon black pepper

1 teaspoon dried thyme leaves

4 cups onions, sliced

1 tablespoons cornstarch

1¼ cups beef stock

Preparation:

1. Season chicken with oil, salt, seasoning, and black pepper. 2. Place the chicken in the Pro-Heat Pan. 3. Install the Accessory Frame in top level of the oven, then place the Pro-Heat Pan on top of it. Close the door. 4. Select BROIL. Set the temperature to 500°F and set the time to 15 minutes. Press START/STOP to begin cooking, flipping the sides after half time. 5. Meanwhile, in a skillet over medium heat, warm the butter and add in remaining ingredients and let it come to a simmer, stir occasionally. Let simmer until onions are tender. 6. Once chicken is done, remove the chicken to a serving dish. Pour the onion sauce over it and enjoy!

Serving Suggestions: Serve with French bread.

Variation Tip: You can use any cheese slice.

Nutritional Information per Serving:

Calories: 561|Fat: 22g|Sat Fat: 9g|Carbohydrates: 52g|Fiber: 3g|Sugar: 10g|Protein: 39g

Classic Ranch Chicken Thigh

Prep Time: 10 minutes | Cook Time: 20 minutes | Servings: 8

 Ingredients:

1 packet ranch seasoning
8 chicken thighs
1 teaspoon garlic powder
1 tablespoon dried chives

1 teaspoons onion powder
1 teaspoon paprika
Olive oil cooking spray

 Preparation:

1. Install the Accessory Frame in the bottom level of the unit. Turn left-hand dial to select BAKE. Set the temperature to 400°F and set the time to 20 minutes. Select START/STOP to begin preheating. 2. In a large bowl, combine all ingredients except for chicken thighs. 3. Mix well and marinade chicken thighs with this mixture. Set aside for 2 hours. 4. Place the chicken in the Pro-Heat Pan. 5. When unit is preheated and ADD FOOD and PRS STRT is displayed, open the door, place the pan in the unit. Close the door and select START/ STOP to begin cooking, flipping each side after half time. 6. Serve and enjoy!

Serving Suggestions: Serve with ranch sauce.
Variation Tip: You can add dried basil leaves for taste variation.
Nutritional Information per Serving:
Calories: 287|Fat: 10.9g|Sat Fat: 3g|Carbohydrates: 0.7g|Fiber: 0.2g|Sugar: 0.2g|Protein: 42.2g

Tandoori Lemon Chicken Legs

Prep Time: 15 minutes | Cook Time: 20 minutes | Servings: 4

 Ingredients:

4 chicken legs
3 tablespoons lemon juice
3 teaspoons ginger paste
3 teaspoons garlic paste
Salt to taste
4 tablespoons yogurt
2 tablespoons tandoori masala powder

2 teaspoons red chili powder
1 teaspoon garam masala powder
1 teaspoon ground cumin
1 teaspoon ground coriander
1 teaspoon ground turmeric
Pepper to taste
Pinch of orange food color

Preparation:

1. Combine all ingredients except for chicken legs in a large bowl. Stir to mix well. 2. Add the chicken legs to the mixture and toss to coat well. Marinated in the refrigerator for 5 hours. 3. Install the Accessory Frame in top level of the oven, then place the Pro-Heat Pan on top of it. Place the Roast Rack in the pan. 4. Place the marinated chicken legs in the Roast Rack and close the door. 5. While holding the smoke box open, use the pellet scoop to pour pellets into the smoke box until filled to the top. Then close the smoke box. 6. Turn dial to select SMOKER, set the temperature to 500°F, and set the time to 20 minutes. Select START/STOP to begin cooking. Flip halfway through the cooking time. 7. Serve and enjoy!

Serving Suggestions: Can be served with rice.
Variation Tip: You can skip the food color if you want.
Nutritional Information per Serving:
Calories: 32 | Fat: 0.9g | Sat Fat: 0.3g | Carbohydrates: 4.3g | Fiber: 0.9g | Sugar: 1.5g | Protein: 1.7g

Chapter 5 Beef, Pork, and Lamb Recipes

Roasted Sweet and Sour Pork Chops

Prep Time: 15 minutes | Cook Time: 15 minutes | Servings: 6

 Ingredients:

6 pork loin chops
1 tablespoon meat tenderizer
Salt and black pepper, to taste
2 garlic cloves, minced

2 tablespoons honey
2 tablespoons soy sauce
1 tablespoon balsamic vinegar
¼ teaspoon ground ginger

 Preparation:

1. Season the pork chops with salt, meat tenderizer, and black pepper. 2. In a large bowl, mix together the remaining ingredients and coat pork chops with this marinade. Cover and refrigerate for about 8 hours. 3. Arrange the marinated pork chops in the Pro-Heat Pan. 4. Install the Accessory Frame in the bottom of the oven, then place the Pro-Heat Pan on top of it. Close the door. 5. While holding the smoke box open, use the pellet scoop to pour pellets into the smoke box until filled to the top. Then close the smoke box. 6. Turn dial to select SMOKER, set the temperature to 450°F, and set the time to 15 minutes. Select START/STOP to begin cooking. Flip halfway through the cooking time. 7. Dish out and serve warm.

Serving Suggestions: Serve these pork chops with rice.
Variation Tip: Bring the pork ribs to room temperature before cooking.
Nutritional Information per Serving:
Calories: 282 | Fat: 19.9g | Sat Fat: 7.5g | Carbohydrates: 6.6g | Fiber: 0.1g | Sugar: 5.9g | Protein: 18.4g

Herbed Garlic Pork Chops

Prep Time: 15 minutes | Cook Time: 15 minutes | Servings: 4

 Ingredients:

½ tablespoon fresh cilantro, chopped
½ tablespoon fresh parsley, chopped
2 tablespoons olive oil
1 tablespoon ground coriander
Salt, to taste

2 (6-ounces) (1-inch thick) pork chops
2 garlic cloves, minced
½ tablespoon fresh rosemary, chopped
¾ tablespoon Dijon mustard
1 teaspoon sugar

 Preparation:

1. In a bowl, mix together the garlic, oil, mustard, herbs, sugar, coriander, and salt. 2. Add pork chops to the bowl generously coat with the marinade. Cover and refrigerate for 3 hours. 3. Arrange the pork ribs in the Pro-Heat Pan. Install the Accessory Frame in the bottom of the oven, then place the Pro-Heat Pan on top of it. Close the door. 4. While holding the smoke box open, use the pellet scoop to pour pellets into the smoke box until filled to the top. Then close the smoke box. 5. Turn dial to select SMOKER, set the temperature to 450°F, and set the time to 15 minutes. Select START/STOP to begin cooking. Flip halfway through the cooking time. 6. Dole out in a platter and serve warm.

Serving Suggestions: Serve these pork chops with curried potato salad.
Variation Tip: You can add basil instead of rosemary.
Nutritional Information per Serving:
Calories: 342 | Fat: 28.3g | Sat Fat: 9g | Carbohydrates: 2g | Fiber: 0.3g | Sugar: 1.1g | Protein: 19.4g

BBQ Roasted Pork Ribs

Prep Time: 10 minutes | Cook Time: 20 minutes | Servings: 4

 **Ingredients:**

¼ cup honey, divided
¾ cup BBQ sauce
2 tablespoons tomato ketchup
1 tablespoon Worcestershire sauce

1 tablespoon soy sauce
½ teaspoon garlic powder
White pepper, to taste
1¾ pounds pork ribs

 **Preparation:**

1. In a bowl, combine 3 tablespoons of honey and the remaining ingredients except pork ribs. 2. Add the pork ribs to the honey mixture and toss until well coated. Marinate in the refrigerator for about 30 minutes. 3. Arrange the marinated pork ribs in the Pro-Heat Pan. 4. Install the Accessory Frame in the bottom of the oven, then place the Pro-Heat Pan on top of it. Close the door. 5. While holding the smoke box open, use the pellet scoop to pour pellets into the smoke box until filled to the top. Then close the smoke box. 6. Turn dial to select SMOKER, set the temperature to 450°F, and set the time to 20 minutes. Select START/STOP to begin cooking. Flip halfway through the cooking time. 7. When cook time is complete, use oven mitts to remove food from the oven, drizzle with the remaining honey and serve warm.

Serving Suggestions: You can serve them with fresh baby greens.
Variation Tip: You can use fresh garlic too instead of garlic powder.
Nutritional Information per Serving:
Calories: 691 | Fat: 35.3g | Sat Fat: 12.5g | Carbohydrates: 37.7g | Fiber: 0.4g | Sugar: 32.2g | Protein: 53.1g

Tasty Garlic Lamb Leg Roast

Prep Time: 20 minutes | Cook Time: 1 hour 20 minutes | Servings: 8

 **Ingredients:**

2¾ pounds lamb leg roast
3 garlic cloves, cut into thin slices
2 tablespoons extra-virgin olive oil

1 tablespoon dried rosemary, crushed
Salt and black pepper, to taste

 Preparation:

1. Mix together the oil, salt, rosemary, and black pepper in a small bowl. 2. Carve deep slits on the top of lamb roast with the tip of a sharp knife. Insert the garlic slices in it. 3. Rub the lamb roast evenly with the oil mixture and place the lamb roast in the Roast Rack. 4. Install the Accessory Frame in top level of the oven, then place the Pro-Heat Pan on top of it. Place the Roast Rack in the pan. Close the door. 5. Select BROIL. Set the temperature to 400°F and set the time to 80 minutes. Press START/STOP to begin cooking. Flip halfway through the cooking time. 6. Dish out and serve warm.

Serving Suggestions: Serve with chopped parsley on top.
Variation Tip: You can add cayenne pepper for taste.
Nutritional Information per Serving:
Calories: 351 | Fat: 17.9g | Sat Fat: 5.6g | Carbohydrates: 0.6g | Fiber: 0.2g | Sugar: 0g | Protein: 44.3g

Spiced Garlic Lamb Steaks

Prep Time: 15 minutes | Cook Time: 20 minutes | Servings: 3

 Ingredients:

5 garlic cloves, peeled
1 teaspoon garam masala
½ teaspoon ground cumin
½ teaspoon cayenne pepper
1½ pounds boneless lamb sirloin steaks

½ onion, roughly chopped
1 tablespoon fresh ginger, peeled
1 teaspoon ground fennel
½ teaspoon ground cinnamon
Salt and black pepper, to taste

 Preparation:

1. Combine the onion, ginger, garlic, and spices in a blender and pulse until smooth. 2. Transfer the mixture to a large bowl and add the lamb steaks. Coat generously with the mixture and refrigerate for 12-24 hours. 3. Then, arrange the lamb steaks in the Pro-Heat Pan. 4. Install the Accessory Frame in the bottom of the oven, then place the Pro-Heat Pan on top of it. Close the door. 5. While holding the smoke box open, use the pellet scoop to pour pellets into the smoke box until filled to the top. Then close the smoke box. 6. Turn dial to select SMOKER, set the temperature to 450°F, and set the time to 20 minutes. Select START/STOP to begin cooking. Flip halfway through the cooking time. 7. Dole out in a platter and cut into desired-sized slices. Serve warm.

Serving Suggestions: Serve with roasted vegetables.
Variation Tip: You can also add white pepper to taste.
Nutritional Information per Serving:
Calories: 222 | Fat: 9.8g | Sat Fat: 3.6g | Carbohydrates: 5.6g | Fiber: 1.3g | Sugar: 0.9g | Protein: 26.6g

Honey Glazed Pork Shoulder

Prep Time: 15 minutes | Cook Time: 20 minutes | Servings: 6

 Ingredients:

⅓ cup soy sauce
2 tablespoons sugar

1 tablespoon honey
2 pounds pork shoulder, cut into 1½-inch thick slices

 Preparation:

1. In a bowl, mix together the sugar, soy sauce, and honey. 2. Add the pork to the soy sauce mixture and toss until well coated. Cover and refrigerate to marinate for 6 hours. 3. Arrange the marinated pork shoulder in the Pro-Heat Pan. 4. Install the Accessory Frame in top level of the oven, then place the Pro-Heat Pan on top of it. Close the door. 5. Select BROIL. Set the temperature to 500°F and set the time to 20 minutes. Press START/STOP to begin cooking. Flip halfway through the cooking time. 6. Dish out in a platter and carve into desired-sized slices, serve warm.

Serving Suggestions: Enjoy this glazed pork shoulder with grilled potatoes.
Variation Tip: Coconut aminos can replace soy sauce in this recipe for low carb diet.
Nutritional Information per Serving:
Calories: 475 | Fat: 32.4g | Sat Fat: 11.9g | Carbohydrates: 8g | Fiber: 0.1g | Sugar: 7.1g | Protein: 36.1g

Crispy Bacon Wrapped Pork Tenderloin

Prep Time: 15 minutes | Cook Time: 20 minutes | Servings: 4

Ingredients:

1 (1½ pound) pork tenderloins
4 bacon strips

2 tablespoons Dijon mustard

Preparation:

1. Spread Dijon mustard evenly over pork tenderloin. 2. Wrap tenderloin in bacon strips. 3. Arrange the pork tenderloin in the Pro-Heat Pan. 4. Install the Accessory Frame in top level of the oven, then place the Pro-Heat Pan on top of it. Close the door. 5. Select BROIL. Set the temperature to400 °F and set the time to 20 minutes. Press START/STOP to begin cooking, flipping once in between. 6. Serve warm.

Serving Suggestions: Serve with mashed potatoes.
Variation Tip: You can omit Dijon mustard from this recipe.
Nutritional Information per Serving:
Calories: 447 | Fat: 23.1g | Sat Fat: 8g | Carbohydrates: 0.4g | Fiber: 0.3g | Sugar: 0.1g | Protein: 55.1g

Baked Pork Loin with Potatoes

Prep Time: 15 minutes | Cook Time: 25 minutes | Servings: 6

Ingredients:

3 tablespoons olive oil, divided
2 pounds pork loin
1 teaspoon fresh parsley, chopped
3 large red potatoes, chopped

½ teaspoon red pepper flakes, crushed
Salt and black pepper, to taste
½ teaspoon garlic powder

Preparation:

1. Install the Accessory Frame in the bottom level of the unit. Turn left-hand dial to select BAKE. Set the temperature to 325°F and set the time to 25 minutes. Select START/STOP to begin preheating. 2. Brush the pork loin with oil rub evenly with salt, parsley, and black pepper. 3. In a large bowl, mix together the potatoes, remaining oil, red pepper flakes, garlic powder, salt, and black pepper and toss until well coated. 4. Place loin in the Pro-Heat Pan and arrange potatoes around it. 5. When unit is preheated and ADD FOOD and PRS STRT is displayed, open the door, place the pan in the unit. Close the door and select START/ STOP to begin cooking. Flip halfway through the cooking time. 6. Dish out in a platter and serve warm.

Serving Suggestions: Serve with other stir-fried vegetables in addition to potatoes.
Variation Tip: You can add white pepper for taste variation.
Nutritional Information per Serving:
Calories: 556 | Fat: 28.3g | Sat Fat: 9g | Carbohydrates: 29.6g | Fiber: 3.2g | Sugar: 1.9g | Protein: 44.9g

Smoked Glazed Ham

Prep Time: 15 minutes | Cook Time: 35 minutes | Servings: 4

 **Ingredients:**

1 cup whiskey

1-pound ham

2 tablespoons French mustard

2 tablespoons honey

 Preparation:

1. Mix together the mustard, whiskey, and honey in a bowl. 2. Trickle the ham with half of the honey mixture and toss to coat well. 3. Arrange the ham in the Pro-Heat Pan. 4. Install the Accessory Frame in the bottom of the oven, then place the Pro-Heat Pan on top of it. Close the door. 5. While holding the smoke box open, use the pellet scoop to pour pellets into the smoke box until filled to the top. Then close the smoke box. 6. Turn dial to select SMOKER, set the temperature to 450°F, and set the time to 15 minutes. Select START/STOP to begin cooking. 7. When cooking time is up, flip the ham and brush with the remaining honey mixture and cook for 20 minutes more. 8. Dish out and serve hot.

Serving Suggestions: Serve with fries or rice.

Variation Tip: You can add maple syrup instead of honey for a different deliciousness.

Nutritional Information per Serving:

Calories: 356 | Fat: 9.8g | Sat Fat: 3.3g | Carbohydrates: 13.1g | Fiber: 1.5g | Sugar: 8.7g | Protein: 18.9g

Yummy Nut Crusted Rack of Lamb

Prep Time: 15 minutes | Cook Time: 25 minutes | Servings: 5

 Ingredients:

1 tablespoon olive oil

1 garlic clove, minced

Salt and black pepper, as required

1¾ pounds rack of lamb

1 egg, beaten

1 tablespoon breadcrumbs

3 ounces pistachios, finely chopped

 Preparation:

1. In a bowl, mix together the garlic, olive oil, salt, and black pepper. Coat the rack of lamb evenly with the oil mixture. 2. In another bowl, mix together the breadcrumbs and pistachios. Dip the rack of lamb in the egg and coat with the pistachio mixture. 3. Arrange the rack of lamb in the Roast Rack. 4. Install the Accessory Frame in top level of the oven, then place the Pro-Heat Pan on top of it. Place the Roast Rack in the pan. Close the door. 5. While holding the smoke box open, use the pellet scoop to pour pellets into the smoke box until filled to the top. Then close the smoke box. 6. Turn dial to select SMOKER, set the temperature to 450°F, and set the time to 25 minutes. Select START/STOP to begin cooking. Flip halfway through the cooking time, flipping once in between. 7. When cook time is complete, use oven mitts to remove food from the oven. Cut into desired-sized slices and serve warm.

Serving Suggestions: Serve with stir-fried vegetables.

Variation Tip: You can also use almonds in this recipe.

Nutritional Information per Serving:

Calories: 362 | Fat: 23.7g | Sat Fat: 5.7g | Carbohydrates: 5.8g | Fiber: 1.8g | Sugar: 1.3g | Protein: 32.3g

Homemade Herbed Lamb Chops

Prep Time: 10 minutes | Cook Time: 12 minutes | Servings: 4

 Ingredients:

1 tablespoon fresh lemon juice
1 tablespoon olive oil
1 teaspoon dried rosemary
1 teaspoon dried thyme
1 teaspoon dried oregano

½ teaspoon ground cumin
½ teaspoon ground coriander
Salt and black pepper, to taste
4 (4-ounces) lamb chops

 Preparation:

1. In a large bowl, mix together the oil, lemon juice, herbs, and spices. 2. Add the chops to the herb mixture and toss until well coated. Marinate in the refrigerator for about 1 hour. 3. Arrange the marinated lamb chops in the Roast Rack. 4. Install the Accessory Frame in top level of the oven, then place the Pro-Heat Pan on top of it. Place the Roast Rack in the pan. Close the door. 5. While holding the smoke box open, use the pellet scoop to pour pellets into the smoke box until filled to the top. Then close the smoke box. 6. Turn dial to select SMOKER, set the temperature to 450°F, and set the time to 12 minutes. Select START/STOP to begin cooking. Flip halfway through the cooking time. 7. Dole out in a platter and serve warm.

Serving Suggestions: Serve it with hummus.
Variation Tip: You can also add some red chili flakes.
Nutritional Information per Serving:
Calories: 246 | Fat: 12g | Sat Fat: 3.5g | Carbohydrates: 0.8g | Fiber: 0.4g | Sugar: 0.1g | Protein: 32g

Garlic Lemon Lamb Chops

Prep Time: 10 minutes | Cook Time: 20 minutes | Servings: 8

 Ingredients:

3 garlic cloves, crushed
1 tablespoon fresh lemon juice
1 teaspoon olive oil

1 tablespoon Za'atar
Salt and black pepper, to taste
8 (3½-ounces) lamb loin chops, bone-in and trimmed

Preparation:

1. Mix together the garlic, lemon juice, oil, Za'atar, salt, and black pepper in a large bowl. 2. Add in the chops and generously coat with the mixture. 3. Arrange chops into the Roast Rack. Install the Accessory Frame in top level of the oven, then place the Pro-Heat Pan on top of it. Place the Roast Rack in the pan. Close the door. 4. Select BROIL. Set the temperature to 450°F and set the time to 20 minutes. Press START/STOP to begin cooking. Flip halfway through the cooking time. 5. Dish out in a platter and serve warm.

Serving Suggestions: Serve with some lemon juice on top.
Variation Tip: You can also use pork chops in this recipe.
Nutritional Information per Serving:
Calories: 192 | Fat: 7.9g | Sat Fat: 2.7g | Carbohydrates: 0.4g | Fiber: 0g | Sugar: 0.1g | Protein: 28g

Classic Pesto Coated Rack of Lamb

Prep Time: 15 minutes | Cook Time: 25 minutes | Servings: 4

 Ingredients:

½ bunch fresh mint
1 garlic clove
¼ cup extra-virgin olive oil

½ tablespoon honey
Salt and black pepper, as required
1 (1½-pounds) rack of lamb

 Preparation:

1. To make the pesto, combine the mint, garlic, honey, oil, salt, and black pepper in a blender and pulse until smooth. 2. Rub the rack of lamb evenly with the pesto. 3. Arrange the rack of lamb in the Roast Rack. 4. Install the Accessory Frame in top level of the oven, then place the Pro-Heat Pan on top of it. Place the Roast Rack in the pan and close the door. 5. While holding the smoke box open, use the pellet scoop to pour pellets into the smoke box until filled to the top. Then close the smoke box. 6. Turn dial to select SMOKER, set the temperature to 450°F, and set the time to 25 minutes. Select START/STOP to begin cooking. Flip halfway through the cooking time. Flip halfway through the cooking time. 7. Dole out in a platter and serve warm.

Serving Suggestions: Serve with boiled potatoes.
Variation Tip: You can also add some fresh parsley.
Nutritional Information per Serving:
Calories: 410 | Fat: 27.7g | Sat Fat: 7.1g | Carbohydrates: 3.9g | Fiber: 1.2g | Sugar: 2.2g | Protein: 35.1g

Baked Herbed Lamb Leg

Prep Time: 15 minutes | Cook Time: 1 hour 15 minutes | Servings: 5

 Ingredients:

2 pounds bone-in leg of lamb
2 tablespoons olive oil
Salt and black pepper, to taste

2 fresh rosemary sprigs
2 fresh thyme sprigs

 Preparation:

1. Install the Accessory Frame in the bottom level of the unit. 2. Turn left-hand dial to select BAKE. Set the temperature to 325°F and set the time to 75 minutes. Select START/STOP to begin preheating. 3. Brush the leg of lamb with oil and season with salt and black pepper. 4. Wrap herb sprigs around the leg of lamb and place the leg of lamb in the Pro-Heat Pan. 5. When unit is preheated and ADD FOOD and PRS STRT is displayed, open the door, place the pan in the unit. Close the door and select START/ STOP to begin cooking. Flip halfway through the cooking time. 6. When cook time is complete, use oven mitts to remove food from the oven. Let it rest and cut the leg of lamb into desired size pieces and serve warm.

Serving Suggestions: Serve with cilantro leaves on top.
Variation Tip: You can also drizzle the leg of lamb with BBQ sauce.
Nutritional Information per Serving:
Calories: 292 | Fat: 13.7g | Sat Fat: 4.1g | Carbohydrates: 0.6g | Fiber: 0.4g | Sugar: 0g | Protein: 37g

Lamb Chops with Mint

Prep Time: 15 minutes | Cook Time: 8 minutes | Servings: 4

 Ingredients:

1 tablespoon fresh mint leaves, chopped
½ teaspoon garlic paste
½ teaspoon ground allspice
¼ teaspoon ground nutmeg
¼ teaspoon ground green cardamom

¼ teaspoon hot paprika
Salt and ground black pepper, as required
2 tablespoons olive oil
1 tablespoon fresh lemon juice
1 rack of lamb, trimmed and separated into 8 chops

 Preparation:

1. In a large bowl, combine all the ingredients except for chops and stir to mix well. 2. Add in the chops and coat with the mixture generously. Marinate in the refrigerator for about 5-6 hours. 3. Then arrange the lamb chops in the Pro-Heat Pan. 4. Install the Accessory Frame in top level of the oven, then place the Pro-Heat Pan on top of it. Close the door. 5. While holding the smoke box open, use the pellet scoop to pour pellets into the smoke box until filled to the top. Then close the smoke box. 6. Turn dial to select SMOKER, set the temperature to 500°F, and set the time to 8 minutes. Select START/STOP to begin cooking. Flip halfway through the cooking time. 7. Once done, serve hot.

Serving Suggestions: Serve alongside the greens of your choice.
Variation Tip: Separate the rack of lamb into equal-sized chops.
Nutritional Information per Serving:
Calories: 368 | Fat: 20.4g | Sat Fat: 0.1g | Carbohydrates: 0.6g | Fiber: 0.2g | Sugar: 0.1g | Protein: 42.7g

Broiled Beef with Potatoes

Prep Time: 15 minutes | Cook Time: 1 hour | Servings: 6

Ingredients:

For Seasoning:
2 teaspoons thyme leaves dried
2 teaspoons sea salt
1 teaspoon black pepper
1 teaspoon garlic powder
1 teaspoon onion powder
2 tablespoons avocado oil or any oil you like

4 lbs. beef chuck roast
1 onion
4 cups beef stock divided
6 carrots, roasted
6 small potatoes, baked

Preparation:

1. Combine all of the ingredients in a bowl and stir until well combined. Then transfer the mixture to the Pro-Heat Pan. 2. Install the Accessory Frame in top level of the oven, then place the Pro-Heat Pan on top of it. Close the door. 3. Select BROIL. Set the temperature to 425°F and set the time to 1 hour. Press START/STOP to begin cooking, flipping sides every 15 minutes. 4. Serve and enjoy.

Serving Suggestions: Serve with baked potatoes and roasted carrots.
Variation Tip: You can also add some cayenne pepper.
Nutritional Information per Serving:
Calories: 658|Fat: 31g|Sat Fat: 12g|Carbohydrates: 44g|Fiber: 6g|Sugar: 6g|Protein: 52g

Savory Lemon Pork Kabobs

Prep Time: 15 minutes | Cook Time: 12 minutes | Servings: 5

 Ingredients:

¼ cup extra-virgin olive oil
3 tablespoons lemon juice
2 tablespoons red wine vinegar
3 garlic cloves, minced
1 tablespoon fresh thyme, chopped

1 tablespoon fresh oregano, chopped
1 teaspoon lemon zest, grated
Salt and ground black pepper, as required
1½ pounds pork tenderloin, cut into 1-inch cubes

 Preparation:

1. In a large bowl, combine all the ingredients except for pork cubes and stir to mix well. 2. Add in the pork cubes and toss until well coated. 3. Cover the bowl and marinate in the refrigerator overnight. 4. Then set the marinated pork on skewers and arrange them in the Pro-Heat Pan. 5. Install the Accessory Frame in top level of the oven, then place the Pro-Heat Pan on top of it. Close the door. 6. While holding the smoke box open, use the pellet scoop to pour pellets into the smoke box until filled to the top. Then close the smoke box. 7. Turn dial to select SMOKER, set the temperature to 450°F, and set the time to 12 minutes. Select START/STOP to begin cooking. 8. Flip the skewers every 3 minutes. 9. When cook time is complete, serve hot.

Serving Suggestions: Serve with a drizzling of lemon juice.
Variation Tip: Use uniform-size pork cubes.
Nutritional Information per Serving:
Calories: 292 | Fat: 15.1g | Sat Fat: 3.2g | Carbohydrates: 1.9g | Fiber: 0.7g | Sugar: 0.3g | Protein: 36g

Lamb Loin Chops with Lemon Juice

Prep Time: 15 minutes | Cook Time: 20 minutes | Servings: 6

 Ingredients:

2 tablespoons Dijon mustard
1 tablespoon fresh lemon juice
½ teaspoon olive oil

1 teaspoon dried tarragon
Salt and black pepper, as required
8 (4-ounces) lamb loin chops

 Preparation:

1. Mix together the mustard, oil, tarragon, lemon juice, salt, and black pepper in a large bowl. 2. Add in the lamb chops and toss until well coated. 3. Arrange the chops in the Pro-Heat Pan. 4. Install the Accessory Frame in top level of the oven, then place the Pro-Heat Pan on top of it. Close the door. 5. Select BROIL. Set the temperature to 425°F and set the time to 20 minutes. Press START/STOP to begin cooking. Flip halfway through the cooking time. 6. Dole out in a platter to serve warm.

Serving Suggestions: You can serve it over cooked basmati rice.
Variation Tip: You can also make this recipe with pork chops.
Nutritional Information per Serving:
Calories: 217|Fat: 8.8g|Sat Fat: 3g|Carbohydrates: 0.3g|Fiber: 0.2g|Sugar: 0.1g|Protein: 32.1g

Healthy Pork & Carrot Burgers

Prep Time: 15 minutes | Cook Time: 14 minutes | Servings: 4

 **Ingredients:**

1-pound ground pork
1 small carrot, peeled and finely chopped
1 large onion, finely chopped
1 tablespoon garlic, minced

2 medium eggs
¼ cup breadcrumbs
1 tablespoon Worcestershire sauce

Preparation:

1. Mix together all ingredients in a bowl and place the mixture in the refrigerator for one hour. 2. Make desired-sized patties from the mixture. 3. Arrange the patties in the lightly greased Pro-Heat Pan. Gently press down the patties with your hands. 4. Install the Accessory Frame in top level of the oven, then place the Pro-Heat Pan on top of it. Close the door. 5. While holding the smoke box open, use the pellet scoop to pour pellets into the smoke box until filled to the top. Then close the smoke box. 6. Turn dial to select SMOKER, set the temperature to 450°F, and set the time to 14 minutes. Select START/STOP to begin cooking. Flip halfway through the cooking time. 7. When cook time is complete, serve hot.

Serving Suggestions: Serve over the hamburger buns.
Variation Tip: Use breadcrumbs of your choice.
Nutritional Information per Serving:
Calories: 247 | Fat: 6.6g | Sat Fat: 2.1g | Carbohydrates: 11.2g | Fiber: 1.5g | Sugar: 3.6g | Protein: 34g

Minty Smoky Lamb Chops

Prep Time: 10 minutes | Cook Time: 20 minutes | Servings: 4

 **Ingredients:**

1½ pounds lamb loin chops, trimmed
1 tablespoon fresh lemon juice
¼ cup fresh parsley, chopped

2 tablespoons fresh mint leaves, chopped
1 tablespoon olive oil
Salt and ground black pepper, as required

Preparation:

1. Combine the lamb loin chops, lemon juice, parsley, mint, oil, salt, and black pepper in a bowl and mix well. 2. Arrange the seasoned lamb chops onto the Roast Rack. 3. Install the Accessory Frame in top level of the oven, then place the Pro-Heat Pan on top of it. Place the Roast Rack in the pan. Close the door. 4. While holding the smoke box open, use the pellet scoop to pour pellets into the smoke box until filled to the top. Then close the smoke box. 5. Turn dial to select SMOKER, set the temperature to 450°F, and set the time to 20 minutes. Select START/STOP to begin cooking. Flip halfway through the cooking time. 6. Once done, serve hot.

Serving Suggestions: Mashed potatoes make a classic pairing with lamb chops.
Variation Tip: Lamb chops that have dried edges and do not smell fresh should not be purchased.
Nutritional Information per Serving:
Calories: 268 | Fat: 16.1g | Sat Fat: 5g | Carbohydrates: 0.6g | Fiber: 0.3g | Sugar: 0.1g | Protein: 48g

Rosemary and Garlic Lamb Chops

Prep Time: 10 minutes | Cook Time: 8 minutes | Servings: 4

 **Ingredients:**

1 garlic clove, minced

1 tablespoon fresh rosemary leaves, minced

Salt and ground black pepper, as required

4 lamb loin chops

 Preparation:

1. Mix together the garlic, salt, rosemary, and black pepper in a bowl and stir to mix well. 2. Rub the lamb chops with the herb mixture generously. 3. Then arrange the lamb chops onto the Roast Rack. 4. Install the Accessory Frame in top level of the oven, then place the Pro-Heat Pan on top of it. Place the Roast Rack in the pan. Close the door. 5. While holding the smoke box open, use the pellet scoop to pour pellets into the smoke box until filled to the top. Then close the smoke box. 6. Turn dial to select SMOKER, set the temperature to 500°F, and set the time to 8 minutes. Select START/STOP to begin cooking. Flip halfway through the cooking time. 7. Once done, serve hot.

Serving Suggestions: Serve the chops with grilled zucchini.

Variation Tip: Lamb chops should contain just the right amount of marbling.

Nutritional Information per Serving:

Calories: 295 | Fat: 10.5g | Sat Fat: 3.8g | Carbohydrates: 2.8g | Fiber: 0.4g | Sugar: 0g | Protein: 41.9g

Lemon & Oregano Lamb Chops

Prep Time: 10 minutes | Cook Time: 9 minutes | Servings: 4

 **Ingredients:**

¼ cup olive oil

2 tablespoons fresh lemon juice

2 tablespoons fresh oregano, chopped

1 teaspoon garlic, minced

Salt and ground black pepper, as required

4 (8-ounce) (½-inch-thick) lamb shoulder blade chops

 Preparation:

1. To make the marinade, add all ingredients to a bowl and stir until well combined. 2. Place the lamb chops and marinade in a large ziplock plastic bag. 3. Seal and shake vigorously to coat evenly with marinade. Let stand at room temperature about 1 hour. 4. Remove chops from the bag and discard marinade. 5. Pat lamb chops dry with paper towels and season lamb chops with a pinch of salt. 6. Arrange the lamb chops onto the Roast Rack. 7. Install the Accessory Frame in top level of the oven, then place the Pro-Heat Pan on top of it. Place the Roast Rack in the pan. Close the door. 8. While holding the smoke box open, use the pellet scoop to pour pellets into the smoke box until filled to the top. Then close the smoke box. 9. Turn dial to select SMOKER, set the temperature to 500°F, and set the time to 9 minutes. Select START/STOP to begin cooking. Flip halfway through the cooking time. 10. Once done, serve hot.

Serving Suggestions: Serve with yogurt sauce.

Variation Tip: Allow the lamb chops to reach room temperature before cooking.

Nutritional Information per Serving:

Calories: 459 | Fat: 31g | Sat Fat: 7.9g | Carbohydrates: 1.8g | Fiber: 1g | Sugar: 0.3g | Protein: 44.5g

Tangy Balsamic Lamb Chops

Prep Time: 10 minutes | Cook Time: 8 minutes | Servings: 8

 Ingredients:

¼ cup olive oil

¼ cup balsamic vinegar

2 tablespoons fresh lemon juice

3-4 garlic cloves, minced

2 teaspoons dried rosemary, crushed

Salt and ground black pepper, as required

8 (1-inch thick) lamb chops

 Preparation:

1. Mix together the oil, vinegar, garlic, lemon juice, rosemary, salt, and black pepper in a bowl. 2. Add in the lamb chops and toss to coat well. Cover and marinate in the refrigerator for about 4-5 hours. 3. Remove the bowl of chops from the refrigerator and let rest at room temperature for at least 30 minutes. 4. Place the marinated lamb chops in the Pro-Heat Pan. 5. Install the Accessory Frame in top level of the oven, then place the Pro-Heat Pan on top of it. Close the door. 6. While holding the smoke box open, use the pellet scoop to pour pellets into the smoke box until filled to the top. Then close the smoke box. 7. Turn dial to select SMOKER, set the temperature to 450°F, and set the time to 8 minutes. Select START/STOP to begin cooking. Flip halfway through the cooking time. 8. When cook time is complete, use oven mitts to remove food from the oven. Let it rest and serve warm.

Serving Suggestions: Serve alongside the beans salad.

Variation Tip: Don't forget to grease the grill grate.

Nutritional Information per Serving:

Calories: 375 | Fat: 18.8g | Sat Fat: 5.4g | Carbohydrates: 0.5g | Fiber: 0g | Sugar: 0.1g | Protein: 47.9g

Cheesy Meatballs with Parsley

Prep Time: 15 minutes | Cook Time: 12 minutes | Servings: 8

 Ingredients:

2 pounds ground beef

1¼ cups breadcrumbs

¼ cup cheddar cheese, grated

2 eggs

¼ cup fresh parsley, chopped

1 small garlic clove, chopped

1 teaspoon dried oregano, crushed

Salt, to taste

Pepper, to taste

 Preparation:

1. In a bowl, combine all ingredients and mix well. 2. Shape the mixture into 2-inch balls. 3. Place the beef meatballs in the Pro-Heat Pan. 4. Install the Accessory Frame in top level of the oven, then place the Pro-Heat Pan on top of it. Close the door. 5. Select BROIL. Set the temperature to 400°F and set the time to 12 minutes. Press START/STOP to begin cooking. 6. Serve with spaghetti and enjoy.

Serving Suggestions: Serve with grated parmesan cheese on top.

Variation Tip: Add some cayenne pepper to enhance the taste.

Nutritional Information per Serving:

Calories: 741|Fat: 35.8g|Sat Fat: 11.8g|Carbohydrates: 29.1g|Fiber: 1.8g|Sugar: 4.3g|Protein: 72.6g

Garlicky Lemon Lamb Chops

Prep Time: 10 minutes | Cook Time: 6 minutes | Servings: 6

 Ingredients:

4 garlic cloves, minced

1 Serrano pepper, chopped

2 tablespoons fresh rosemary, chopped

¼ teaspoon cayenne powder

Salt and ground black pepper, as required

1 tablespoon fresh lemon juice

2 tablespoons olive oil

6 (6-ounce) (¾-inch thick) lamb chops

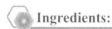 **Preparation:**

1. In a food processor, combine all ingredients except the lamb chops and pulse until paste forms. 2. Transfer the paste to a large bowl and add in the chops; stir until well coated. 3. Cover and refrigerate for at least 1-2 hours. 4. Then remove the bowl of chops from a refrigerator and let rest at room temperature for at least 20 minutes. 5. Place the lamb chops in the Pro-Heat Pan. 6. Install the Accessory Frame in top level of the oven, then place the Pro-Heat Pan on top of it. Close the door. 7. While holding the smoke box open, use the pellet scoop to pour pellets into the smoke box until filled to the top. Then close the smoke box. 8. Turn dial to select SMOKER, set the temperature to 500°F, and set the time to 6 minutes. Select START/STOP to begin cooking. Flip halfway through the cooking time. 9. When cook time is complete, use oven mitts to remove chops from the oven. Let it rest and serve warm.

Serving Suggestions: Serve alongside the yogurt dip.

Variation Tip: Lamb chops with dried-out edges should not be purchased.

Nutritional Information per Serving:

Calories: 363 | Fat: 17.4g | Sat Fat: 5.2g | Carbohydrates: 1.4g | Fiber: 0.6g | Sugar: 0.1g | Protein: 48g

Mustard Rack of Lamb

Prep Time: 15 minutes | Cook Time: 25 minutes | Servings: 8

 Ingredients:

2 (2½-pounds) racks of lamb, chine bones removed and trimmed

Salt and ground black pepper, as required

2 tablespoons Dijon mustard

2 teaspoons fresh rosemary, chopped

2 teaspoons fresh parsley, chopped

2 teaspoons fresh thyme, chopped

 **Preparation:**

1. Season the rack of lamb with salt and pepper. 2. Rub the meaty sides of the lamb with mustard and fresh herbs, pressing gently. 3. Arrange the lamb chops onto the Roast Rack. 4. Install the Accessory Frame in top level of the oven, then place the Pro-Heat Pan on top of it. Place the Roast Rack in the pan. Close the door. 5. While holding the smoke box open, use the pellet scoop to pour pellets into the smoke box until filled to the top. Then close the smoke box. 6. Turn dial to select SMOKER, set the temperature to 500°F, and set the time to 25 minutes. Select START/STOP to begin cooking. Flip halfway through the cooking time. Flip the racks of lamb after every 9 minutes. 7. When cook time is complete, use oven mitts to remove food from the oven. Let it rest on a cutting board for about 10 minutes. 8. Carve the racks of lamb into chops and serve.

Serving Suggestions: Serve alongside the lemon wedges.

Variation Tip: Make sure to remove the silver skin from the rack of lamb.

Nutritional Information per Serving:

Calories: 532 | Fat: 21g | Sat Fat: 7.5g | Carbohydrates: 0.6g | Fiber: 0.4g | Sugar: 0g | Protein: 79.8g

Simple Broiled Lamb Chops

Prep Time: 10 minutes | Cook Time: 20 minutes | Servings: 4

 **Ingredients:**

1 tablespoon olive oil

Salt and black pepper, to taste

4 (4-ounces) lamb chops

 **Preparation:**

1.In a large bowl, mix together the salt, oil, and black pepper. Add in the chops and toss to coat well. 2. Arrange the seasoned chops in the Roast Rack. 3. Install the Accessory Frame in top level of the oven, then place the Pro-Heat Pan on top of it. Place the Roast Rack in the pan. Close the door. 4. Select BROIL. Set the temperature to 390°F and set the time to 20 minutes. Press START/STOP to begin cooking. Flip halfway through the cooking time. 5. Dole out in a platter and serve warm.

Serving Suggestions: You can serve it with fig and arugula salad.

Variation Tip: The addition of dried herbs will add a delish touch in lamb chops.

Nutritional Information per Serving:

Calories: 241 | Fat: 11.8g | Sat Fat: 3.5g | Carbohydrates: 0g | Fiber: 0g | Sugar: 0g | Protein: 31.8g

Grilled Lamb Chops with Apple Sauce

Prep Time: 15 minutes | Cook Time: 12 minutes | Servings: 8

 Ingredients:

Apple Sauce:

3 sprigs parsley leaves

½ cup mint leaves

1 apple, sliced and cored

Lamb Chops:

¼ cup olive oil

1 rack of lamb

3 cloves garlic, minced

1 tablespoon lemon juice

⅓ cup olive oil

Salt and black pepper, to taste

2 teaspoons rosemary, chopped

 Preparation:

1. In a blender, combine all the ingredients of apple sauce and blend well. 2. Pour the apple sauce into a jar and refrigerate. 3. In a large bowl, combine all the lamb marinade ingredients and mix well. 4. Slice rack of lambs into chops and add to the marinade bowl; stir until well coated. Marinate for about 30 minutes. 5. Place the marinated lamb in the Pro-Heat Pan. 6. Install the Accessory Frame in top level of the oven, then place the Pro-Heat Pan on top of it. Close the door. 7. While holding the smoke box open, use the pellet scoop to pour pellets into the smoke box until filled to the top. Then close the smoke box. 8. Turn dial to select SMOKER, set the temperature to 450°F, and set the time to 12 minutes. Select START/STOP to begin cooking. Flip halfway through the cooking time. 9. Once done, serve hot.

Serving Suggestions: Serve with apple sauce.

Variation Tip: To add taste variation, you could add dried basil leave.

Nutritional Information per Serving:

Calories: 271 | Fat: 20.3g | Sat Fat: 4.5g | Carbohydrates: 5g | Fiber: 1.2g | Sugar: 3g | Protein: 17.6g

Pork Spare Ribs with Vinegar

Prep Time: 15 minutes | Cook Time: 18 minutes | Servings: 6

 Ingredients:

½ cup rice vinegar
6 garlic cloves, minced
2 tablespoons soy sauce
12 (1-inch) pork spare ribs

2 tablespoons olive oil
Salt and black pepper, to taste
½ cup cornstarch

Preparation:

1. In a large bowl, mix together the garlic, soy sauce, vinegar, salt, and black pepper. 2. Add in the pork ribs and toss to coat well. Marinate in the refrigerator overnight. 3. Then dredge the pork ribs in the cornstarch and drizzle with oil. 4. Place the marinated lamb in the Pro-Heat Pan. 5. Install the Accessory Frame in top level of the oven, then place the Pro-Heat Pan on top of it. Close the door. 6. While holding the smoke box open, use the pellet scoop to pour pellets into the smoke box until filled to the top. Then close the smoke box. 7. Turn dial to select SMOKER, set the temperature to 450°F, and set the time to 18 minutes. Select START/STOP to begin cooking. Flip halfway through the cooking time. 8. Once done, serve hot.

Serving Suggestions: Serve with lemon juice on top.
Variation Tip: You can also use white vinegar instead of rice vinegar.
Nutritional Information per Serving:
Calories: 681 | Fat: 52.7g | Sat Fat: 18.7g | Carbohydrates: 11.2g | Fiber: 0.2g | Sugar: 0.1g | Protein: 34.6g

Grilled Steak with Potato Wedges

Prep Time: 15 minutes | Cook Time: 65 minutes | Servings: 4

 Ingredients:

4 potatoes, boiled and cut into wedges
3 sirloin steak
¼ cup avocado oil

2 tablespoons steak seasoning
1 tablespoon sea salt

 Preparation:

1. Install the Accessory Frame in the bottom level of the unit. Turn left-hand dial to select BAKE. Set the temperature to 400°F and set the time to 20 minutes. Select START/STOP to begin preheating. 2. Place the potato wedges in the Pro-Heat Pan. 3. When unit is preheated and ADD FOOD and PRS STRT is displayed, open the door, place the pan in the unit. Close the door and select START/ STOP to begin cooking. 4. Once done, transfer the potatoes to a bowl and set aside. 5. Season the steak with oil, salt and seasoning. Place the steaks in the Pro-Heat Pan in the unit. 6. While holding the smoke box open, use the pellet scoop to pour pellets into the smoke box until filled to the top. Then close the smoke box. 7. Turn dial to select SMOKER, set the temperature to 400°F, and set the time to 30 minutes. Select START/STOP to begin cooking. Flip halfway through the cooking time. 8. When the cooking time is up, cook them for 15 minutes more. 9. Serve with wedges and enjoy!

Serving Suggestions: Serve with potato wedges.
Variation Tip: Coconut oil can also be used.
Nutritional Information per Serving:
Calories: 572|Fat: 38g|Sat Fat: 12g|Carbohydrates: 21g|Fiber: 4g|Sugar: 1g|Protein: 38g

Beef Stuffed Bell Peppers

Prep Time: 15 minutes | Cook Time: 25 minutes | Servings: 4

 Ingredients:

1 teaspoon olive oil
½ medium onion, chopped
2 garlic cloves, minced
1-pound lean ground beef
1 teaspoon dried dill, crushed
1 teaspoon garlic salt

½ teaspoon red chili powder
½ cup cooked jasmine rice
⅔ cup light Mexican cheese, shredded
1½ can tomato sauce
2 teaspoons Worcestershire sauce
4 bell peppers, tops removed and seeded

 Preparation:

1. Heat the oil in a skillet over medium heat. 2. Stir in the chopped onion and garlic, and cook for 5 minutes. 3. Add in the beef and cook for 10 minutes. 4. Add rice, tomato sauce, cheese, and Worcestershire sauce to a bowl. Stir to mix well. Season with garlic salt and red chili powder. 5. Now fill every bell pepper with the beef mixture and top with the rice mixture. 6. Arrange the stuffed bell peppers in the Pro-Heat Pan. 7. Install the Accessory Frame in top level of the oven, then place the Pro-Heat Pan on top of it. Close the door. 8. Select BROIL. Set the temperature to 400°F and set the time to 8 minutes. Press START/STOP to begin cooking. 9. Sprinkle with the crushed dried dill. Serve warm!

Serving Suggestions: Serve with sprinkling rosemary on top.
Variation Tip: You can add oregano to make taste variation.
Nutritional Information per Serving:
Calories: 439| Fat: 3.1g|Sat Fat: 1.2g|Carbohydrates: 34.4g|Fiber: 2.6g|Sugar: 1.6g|Protein: 11.3g

Yummy Lamb Burgers

Prep Time: 15 minutes | Cook Time: 8 minutes | Servings: 6

 Ingredients:

2 pounds lean ground lamb
1 large onion, finely chopped
2 garlic cloves, minced
1 green chili pepper, seeded and chopped
1 tablespoon fresh cilantro, chopped

2 eggs, beaten
2 teaspoons prepared mustard
1 tablespoon garam masala powder
1 tablespoon dry fenugreek leaves, crushed
Salt, as required

 Preparation:

1. Mix together all ingredients in a bowl and refrigerate for an hour.
Shape the mixture into 12 equal-sized sized patties. 2. Place the patties in the lightly greased Pro-Heat Pan. 3. Install the Accessory Frame in top level of the oven, then place the Pro-Heat Pan on top of it. Close the door. 4. While holding the smoke box open, use the pellet scoop to pour pellets into the smoke box until filled to the top. Then close the smoke box. 5. Turn dial to select SMOKER, set the temperature to 450°F, and set the time to 8 minutes. Select START/STOP to begin cooking. Flip halfway through the cooking time. 6. Once done, serve hot.

Serving Suggestions: Serve with tzatziki sauce.
Variation Tip: For the best result, grind your meat at home.
Nutritional Information per Serving:
Calories: 334 | Fat: 32.2g | Sat Fat: 9.9g | Carbohydrates: 4g | Fiber: 1.1g | Sugar: 1.2g | Protein: 2.7g

Garlicky Leg of Lamb

Prep Time: 15 minutes | Cook Time: 1 hour | Servings: 10

 **Ingredients:**

6 garlic cloves, minced
Salt and ground black pepper, as required
1 teaspoon ground cumin
1 teaspoon ground cinnamon
1 teaspoon ground cardamom

1 teaspoon paprika
½ teaspoon cayenne powder
2 tablespoons olive oil
1 (4-pound) boneless leg of lamb, butterflied and trimmed

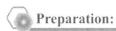 **Preparation:**

1. Mix together the garlic cloves, salt and black pepper in a small bowl. Mash with the back of a spoon until a paste forms. 2. Add the spices and stir to mix well. 3. Place leg of lamb, cut side up, on a smooth surface. 4. Spread ¾ of the mixture in the center, leaving a 1-inch border on each side. 5. Roll up short sides, sealing in spice mixture, and tie in multiple knots with kitchen string to form a soccer ball-like shape. 6. Spread outside of roll with the remaining spice mixture. 7. Loosely cover rolls with plastic wrap; chill in refrigerator at least 2 hours. 8. Place the lamb roll onto the Roast Rack. 9. Install the Accessory Frame in top level of the oven, then place the Pro-Heat Pan on top of it. Place the Roast Rack in the pan. Close the door. 10. While holding the smoke box open, use the pellet scoop to pour pellets into the smoke box until filled to the top. Then close the smoke box. 11. Turn dial to select SMOKER, set the temperature to 450°F, and set the time to 30 minutes. Select START/STOP to begin cooking. Flip halfway through the cooking time. 12. When the cooking time is up, flip the lamb and cook for an additional 30 minutes. 13. Once done, place the lamb roll onto a cutting board and let rest for about 10-20 minutes. 14. Cut the roll into desired size slices and serve.

Serving Suggestions: Serve with steamed cauliflower.
Variation Tip: Look for a leg of lamb with light red meat.
Nutritional Information per Serving:
Calories: 367 | Fat: 16.2g | Sat Fat: 5.2g | Carbohydrates: 1.2g | Fiber: 0.3g | Sugar: 0.1g | Protein: 51.2g

Chapter 6 Fish and Seafood Recipes

Simple Crispy Prawns

Prep Time: 15 minutes | Cook Time: 8 minutes | Servings: 4

 Ingredients:

1 egg

½ pound nacho chips, crushed

18 prawns, peeled and deveined

 Preparation:

1. Crack the egg in a shallow bowl and beat well. 2. Crush nacho chips in another bowl and set aside. 3. Dip the prawn into the egg and then coat it with the nacho chips. 4. Place the coated prawns in the Pro-Heat Pan. 5. Install the Accessory Frame in top level of the oven, then place the Pro-Heat Pan on top of it. Close the door. 6. Select BROIL. Set the temperature to 355°F and set the time to 8 minutes. Press START/STOP to begin cooking, flipping halfway through the cooking time. 7. Serve hot!

Serving Suggestions: Serve with ketchup or tartar sauce.
Variation Tip: You can add seasoned breadcrumbs instead of nachos for coating.
Nutritional Information per Serving:
Calories: 425 | Fat: 17.6g | Sat Fat: 3.1g | Carbohydrates: 36.6g | Fiber: 2.6g | Sugar: 2.2g | Protein: 28.6g

Pretzel-Crushed Catfish Fillets

Prep Time: 15 minutes | Cook Time: 12 minutes | Servings: 4

 Ingredients:

4 catfish fillets

½ teaspoon salt and pepper

2 large eggs

⅓ cup Dijon mustard

2 tablespoons milk

½ cup all-purpose flour

4 cups honey mustard miniature pretzels, coarsely crushed

Cooking spray

 Preparation:

1. Whisk together the eggs, mustard, and milk in a bowl. Place flour in a second bowl and pretzels in the third bowl. 2. Season the catfish with salt and pepper. Coat the fish in the flour first, then dip in egg mixture, and finally coat in pretzels. 3. Place the coated fish in the Roast Rack and spray with oil. 4. Install the Accessory Frame in top level of the oven, then place the Pro-Heat Pan on top of it. Place the Roast Rack in the pan. Close the door. 5. Select BROIL. Set the temperature to 325°F and set the time to 12 minutes. Press START/STOP to begin cooking. 6. When done, serve and enjoy.

Serving Suggestions: Serve with lemon slices.
Variation Tip: You can also serve it with macaroni.
Nutritional Information per Serving:
Calories: 466 | Fat: 14g | Sat Fat: 3g | Carbohydrates: 45g | Fiber: 2g | Sugar: 2g | Protein: 33g

Broiled Salmon with Potatoes

Prep Time: 10 minutes | Cook Time: 18 minutes | Servings: 4

 Ingredients:

1 lb. baby potatoes, halved and baked
Kosher salt to taste
Pepper to taste
1 tablespoon + 1 teaspoon thyme, divided

2 teaspoons rosemary
5 garlic cloves, divided and minced
Extra virgin olive oil, as required
1 lb. salmon fillet

 Preparation:

1. Season the salmon with salt and black pepper. Add in the potatoes. Add in the herbs and stir to mix well. 2. Drizzle 3 tablespoons oil over the fillets and add the garlic on top. 3. Arrange the salmon and potatoes in the Pro-Heat Pan. 4. Install the Accessory Frame in top level of the oven, then place the Pro-Heat Pan on top of it. Close the door. 5. Select BROIL. Set the temperature to 450°F and set the time to 18 minutes. Press START/STOP to begin cooking, tossing once in between. 6. Dish out and drizzle with the lemon juice, serve and enjoy.

Serving Suggestions: Serve with fresh thyme and rosemary on top.
Variation Tip: You can add white pepper.
Nutritional Information per Serving:
Calories: 253.9 | Fat: 1.1g | Sat Fat: 0.3g | Carbohydrates: 21g | Fiber: 2.6g | Sugar: 0g | Protein: 25g

Yummy Crispy Coconut Shrimp

Prep Time: 10 minutes | Cook Time: 10 minutes | Servings: 4

 Ingredients:

1-pound shrimp
½ teaspoon salt
½ cup all-purpose flour
1 large egg, beaten

1 cup bread crumbs
½ cup shredded coconut
Olive oil
Cooking spray

 Preparation:

1. Mix flour and salt in a shallow bowl; whisk the egg in a second bowl, and combine the breadcrumbs and coconut in a third bowl. 2. Dredge the shrimp in the flour, then dip into the egg. Finally coat it in the bread crumb mixture. 3. Place the coated shrimp in the Pro-Heat Pan and spray with oil. 4. Install the Accessory Frame in top level of the oven, then place the Pro-Heat Pan on top of it. Close the door. 5. Select BROIL. Set the temperature to 375°F and set the time to 10 minutes. Press START/STOP to begin cooking, tossing them in between. 6. When done, serve and enjoy!

Serving Suggestions: Serve with any sauce.
Variation Tip: You can also top it with fresh cilantro.
Nutritional Information per Serving:
Calories: 294 | Fat: 19g | Sat Fat: 16g | Carbohydrates: 21g | Fiber: 5g | Sugar: 1.8g | Protein: 12g

Garlicky Shrimp with Lemon Juice

Prep Time: 8 minutes | Cook Time: 10 minutes | Servings: 1

 **Ingredients:**

1 garlic clove, minced
½ tablespoon fresh cilantro, chopped
¼ pound shrimp, peeled and deveined

½ tablespoon olive oil
½ teaspoon fresh lemon juice
½ Serrano pepper, seeded and chopped finely

 **Preparation:**

1. Combine the garlic, oil, lemon juice and Serrano pepper in a large bowl. Stir to mix well. 2. Add in the shrimp and toss until well coated. 3. Arrange the shrimp in the Pro-Heat Pan. 4. Install the Accessory Frame in top level of the oven, then place the Pro-Heat Pan on top of it. 5. While holding the smoke box open, use the pellet scoop to pour pellets into the smoke box until filled to the top. Then close the smoke box. 6. Turn dial to select SMOKER, set the temperature to 450°F, and set the time to 10 minutes. Select START/STOP to begin cooking. Flip halfway through the cooking time, turning them occasionally. 7. Once done, top with cilantro and serve.

Serving Suggestions: Serve it with mango salsa.
Variation Tip: You can add red pepper flakes to make spicy garlic shrimp.
Nutritional Information per Serving:
Calories: 201 | Fat: 9g | Sat Fat: 1.6g | Carbohydrates: 3g | Fiber: 0.2g | Sugar: 0.2g | Protein: 26.1g

Honey Salmon Fillet

Prep Time: 10 minutes | Cook Time: 15 minutes | Servings: 6

 **Ingredients:**

2 lb. salmon fillet
Kosher salt to taste
2 tablespoons and ½ teaspoon olive oil
4 tablespoons mustard, whole grain

2 tablespoons honey
4 cloves garlic, minced
1 teaspoon paprika
½ teaspoon black pepper

 **Preparation:**

1. Install the Accessory Frame in the bottom level of the unit. 2. Turn left-hand dial to select BAKE. Set the temperature to 375°F and set the time to 15 minutes. Select START/STOP to begin preheating. 3. Place salmon in a bowl and season with salt and pepper. 4. Add in the olive oil, honey, garlic, mustard, and paprika in a small bowl. Mix well. 5. Then place the salmon in the Pro-Heat Pan. 6. When unit is preheated and ADD FOOD and PRS STRT is displayed, open the door, place the pan in the unit. Close the door and select START/ STOP to begin cooking. 7. Serve and enjoy.

Serving Suggestions: Serve with rice and enjoy.
Variation Tip: You can add cayenne pepper for taste.
Nutritional Information per Serving:
Calories: 292 | Fat: 15.1g | Sat Fat: 2.2g | Carbohydrates: 7.3g | Fiber: 0.6g | Sugar: 2.1g | Protein: 30.7g

Cajun Garlic Cod Filets

Prep Time: 10 minutes | Cook Time: 16 minutes | Servings: 12

 Ingredients:

3 pounds cod
6 tablespoons plantain flour
2 teaspoons smoked paprika
½ cup gluten-free flour

4 teaspoons Cajun seasoning
1 teaspoon garlic powder
Salt and pepper, to taste

Preparation:

1. In a shallow bowl, mix together the plantain flour, gluten-free flour, Cajun seasoning, smoked paprika, garlic powder, salt, and pepper. 2. Roll the fillets in the flour mixture and refrigerate for about 2 hours. 3. Arrange the fillets in the Pro-Heat Pan and shower with olive oil. 4. Install the Accessory Frame in the bottom of the oven, then place the Pro-Heat Pan on top of it. Close the door. 5. While holding the smoke box open, use the pellet scoop to pour pellets into the smoke box until filled to the top. Then close the smoke box. 6. Turn dial to select SMOKER, set the temperature to 450°F, and set the time to 16 minutes. Select START/STOP to begin cooking. Flip halfway through the cooking time. 7. Remove the cod fillets and place them on a serving platter. Enjoy!

Serving Suggestions: Serve with hot sauce.
Variation Tip: You can use regular flour instead.
Nutritional Information per Serving:
Calories: 139 | Fat: 1.1g | Sat Fat: 0.2g | Carbohydrates: 4.4g | Fiber: 0.7g | Sugar: 0.2g | Protein: 26.3g

Herbed Butter Salmon

Prep Time: 5 minutes | Cook Time: 10 minutes | Servings: 3

 Ingredients:

1-pound salmon fillets
2 tablespoons butter
1½ tablespoons brown sugar
½ teaspoon parsley

½ teaspoon garlic powder
½ teaspoon salt
¼ teaspoon pepper

Preparation:

1. In a bowl, mix together the garlic powder, brown sugar, butter, salt, parsley, and pepper. 2. Add in the salmon fillets and toss until well coated. 3. Arrange the salmon in the Pro-Heat Pan and shower with olive oil. 4. Install the Accessory Frame in top level of the oven, then place the Pro-Heat Pan on top of it. Close the door. 5. While holding the smoke box open, use the pellet scoop to pour pellets into the smoke box until filled to the top. Then close the smoke box. 6. Turn dial to select SMOKER, set the temperature to 450°F, and set the time to 10 minutes. Select START/STOP to begin cooking. Flip halfway through the cooking time. 7. When cook time is complete, use oven mitts to remove food from the oven. Let it rest and serve warm.

Serving Suggestions: Serve with chopped mint leaves on the top.
Variation Tip: Use skinless salmon fillets.
Nutritional Information per Serving:
Calories: 333 | Fat: 17g | Sat Fat: 6.2g | Carbohydrates: 16.7g | Fiber: 0.1g | Sugar: 16.1g | Protein: 29.5g

Homemade Salmon Cakes

Prep Time: 10 minutes | Cook Time: 21 minutes | Servings: 4

 Ingredients:

3 teaspoons olive oil, divided
1 small onion, finely chopped
1 stalk celery, finely diced
2 tablespoons chopped fresh parsley
15 ounces canned salmon, drained

1 large egg, lightly beaten
1½ teaspoon Dijon mustard
1¾ cups fresh whole-wheat breadcrumbs
½ teaspoon freshly ground pepper

 Preparation:

1. In a nonstick skillet over medium-high heat, warm the oil. 2. Stir in the onion and celery until they are cooked for about 3 minutes. Remove from the heat and stir in the parsley. 3. Place the salmon in a medium bowl. Use a fork to remove any bones and skin. Flake them apart with a knife. Whisk in the egg and mustard. 4. Stir in the breadcrumbs, onion mixture and pepper. Form the mixture into eight 2½-inch-wide patties. 5. Arrange the patties in the Pro-Heat Pan. 6. Install the Accessory Frame in the bottom level of the unit. Turn left-hand dial to select BAKE. Set the temperature to 400°F and set the time to 18 minutes. Select START/STOP to begin preheating. 7. When unit is preheated and ADD FOOD and PRS STRT is displayed, open the door, place the pan in the unit. Close the door and select START/ STOP to begin cooking. 8. Serve and enjoy!

Serving Suggestions: Serve with creamy dill sauce.
Variation Tip: You can also add cooked salmon.
Nutritional Information per Serving:
Calories: 350 | Fat: 13g | Sat Fat: 1.4g | Carbohydrates: 23g | Fiber: 5g | Sugar: 5g | Protein: 34g

Savory Broiled Salmon

Prep Time: 10 minutes | Cook Time: 10 minutes | Servings: 4

 **Ingredients:**

4 salmon fillets
2 tablespoons olive oil

Salt and black pepper, to taste

Preparation:

1. Season each salmon fillet with salt and pepper, then brush with the oil. 2. Arrange them in the Pro-Heat Pan and shower with cooking oil spray. 3. Install the Accessory Frame in top level of the oven, then place the Pro-Heat Pan on top of it. Close the door. 4. Select BROIL. Set the temperature to 425°F and set the time to 10 minutes. Press START/ STOP to begin cooking, tossing them in between. 5. When cook time is complete, use oven mitts to remove the salmon fillets from the oven. 6. Let it rest and serve warm.

Serving Suggestions: Serve with the garnishing of scallion.
Variation Tip: Use skinless salmon fillets.
Nutritional Information per Serving:
Calories: 285 |Fat: 17.5g|Sat Fat: 2.5g|Carbohydrates: 0g|Fiber: 0g|Sugar: 0g|Protein: 33g

Smoky Lemon Tilapia

Prep Time: 10 minutes | Cook Time: 12 minutes | Servings: 4

 Ingredients:

4 tilapia fillets
1 teaspoon lemon pepper seasoning
1 teaspoon garlic powder

1 teaspoon onion powder
Salt and ground black pepper, as required
2 tablespoons olive oil

 Preparation:

1. In a small bowl, mix the garlic powder, lemon pepper seasoning, onion powder, salt, and black pepper. 2. Brush the tilapia fillets with oil and then rub with the spice mixture. 3. Arrange them in the Pro-Heat Pan. 4. Install the Accessory Frame in the bottom of the oven, then place the Pro-Heat Pan on top of it. Close the door. 5. While holding the smoke box open, use the pellet scoop to pour pellets into the smoke box until filled to the top. Then close the smoke box. 6. Turn dial to select SMOKER, set the temperature to 450°F, and set the time to 12 minutes. Select START/STOP to begin cooking. Flip halfway through the cooking time. 7. Remove the tilapia fillets and place them on a serving platter. Enjoy!

Serving Suggestions: Serve with your favorite salad.
Variation Tip: Use seasoning according to your choice.
Nutritional Information per Serving:
Calories: 206 | Fat: 8.6g | Sat Fat: 1.7g | Carbohydrates: 0.2g | Fiber: 0.1g | Sugar: 0.4g | Protein: 31.9g

Flavorful Salmon with Asparagus

Prep Time: 10 minutes | Cook Time: 15 minutes | Servings: 4

 Ingredients:

4 salmon fillets
3 tablespoons lemon juice
4 tablespoons fresh dill, roughly chopped
2 tablespoons olive oil

4 tablespoons fresh parsley, roughly chopped
2 pounds asparagus
Salt and pepper, to taste

Preparation:

1. In a small bowl, mix together the lemon juice, salt, pepper, olive oil, dill, and parsley. 2. Coat the salmon fillets in the mixture and set aside. 3. Stir in the asparagus and stir to mix well. 4. Arrange them in the Pro-Heat Pan and shower with olive oil. 5. Install the Accessory Frame in the bottom of the oven, then place the Pro-Heat Pan on top of it. Close the door. 6. While holding the smoke box open, use the pellet scoop to pour pellets into the smoke box until filled to the top. Then close the smoke box. 7. Turn dial to select SMOKER, set the temperature to 450°F, and set the time to 15 minutes. Select START/STOP to begin cooking. Flip halfway through the cooking time. 8. When cook time is complete, use oven mitts to remove food from the oven. Let it rest and serve warm.

Serving Suggestions: Serve with lemon wedges on the top.
Variation Tip: Don't use skinless salmon fillets.
Nutritional Information per Serving:
Calories: 296 | Fat: 14.3g | Sat Fat: 2g | Carbohydrates: 6.1g | Fiber: 0.3g | Sugar: 5.7g | Protein: 37g

Tomato & Corn Broiled Tilapia

Prep Time: 10 minutes | Cook Time: 10 minutes | Servings: 4

Ingredients:

1 cup fresh cilantro leaves

1 cup fresh parsley leaves

2 tablespoons olive oil

2 teaspoons grated lemon zest

2 tablespoons lemon juice

1 tablespoon coarsely chopped fresh ginger root

¾ teaspoon sea salt or kosher salt divided

2 cups grape tomatoes, halved lengthwise

1½ cups fresh or frozen corn, thawed

4 tilapia fillets

Preparation:

1. Combine the first 6 ingredients and ½ teaspoon salt in a food processor. Pulse the mixture until finely chopped. 2. In a mixing bowl, combine the tomatoes and corn; add in 1 tablespoon of the herb mixture and the remaining salt. Stir to mix well. 3. Place each fillet on heavy aluminum foil. 4. Using a spoon, pour tomato mixture alongside the fish and spread the herb mixture on top. Wrap the foil securely around the fish and vegetables. 5. Arrange them in the Pro-Heat Pan. Install the Accessory Frame in the bottom of the oven, then place the Pro-Heat Pan on top of it. Close the door. 6. Select BROIL. Set the temperature to 450°F and set the time to 10 minutes. Press START/STOP to begin cooking, turning once in between. 7. Remove and place them on a serving platter. Serve and enjoy!

Serving Suggestions: Served with salad.

Variation Tip: Top with lemon juice.

Nutritional Information per Serving:

Calories: 270 | Fat: 9g | Sat Fat: 2g | Carbohydrates: 15g | Fiber: 4g | Sugar: 9g | Protein: 35g

Easy Broiled Cajun Catfish

Prep Time: 10 minutes | Cook Time: 15 minutes | Servings: 4

Ingredients:

4 catfish fillets

4 tablespoons cornmeal polenta

4 teaspoons Cajun seasoning

1 teaspoon paprika

1 teaspoon garlic powder

Salt, as required

2 tablespoons olive oil

Preparation:

1. In a bowl, mix the cornmeal, paprika, garlic powder, Cajun seasoning, and salt. 2. Add the catfish fillets to the spice mixture and toss until well coated. 3. Brush each fillet with oil and place them in the Pro-Heat Pan. 4. Install the Accessory Frame in top level of the oven, then place the Pro-Heat Pan on top of it. Close the door. 5. Select BROIL. Set the temperature to 425°F and set the time to 15 minutes. Press START/STOP to begin cooking, tossing once in between. 6. Remove the catfish fillets and place them on a serving platter. Enjoy!

Serving Suggestions: Serve with your favorite salad.

Variation Tip: Use the seasoning according to your choice.

Nutritional Information per Serving:

Calories: 321 | Fat: 20.3g | Sat Fat: 3.4g | Carbohydrates: 6.7g | Fiber: 0.3g | Sugar: 0.3g | Protein: 27.3g

Baked Celery-Crab Cakes

Prep Time: 20 minutes | Cook Time: 12 minutes | Servings: 6

 **Ingredients:**

1 medium sweet red pepper, finely chopped
1 celery rib, finely chopped
3 green onions, finely chopped
2 large egg whites
3 tablespoons reduced-fat mayonnaise

¼ teaspoon wasabi, prepared
¼ teaspoon salt
½ cup dry bread crumbs divided
½ cup lump crabmeat, drained
Cooking spray

 Preparation:

1. In a bowl, combine the sweet red pepper, green onions, celery rib, egg whites, wasabi, mayonnaise, salt, and ⅓ cup bread crumbs. Mix well and gently fold in the crab. 2. Shape the crab mixture into ¾-inch thick patties. 3. Place the remaining crumbs in a bowl and gently coat the patties. 4. Arrange the patties in the Pro-Heat Pan and spray with cooking spray. 5. Install the Accessory Frame in the bottom level of the unit. Turn left-hand dial to select BAKE. Set the temperature to 375°F and set the time to 12 minutes. Select START/STOP to begin preheating. 6. When unit is preheated and ADD FOOD and PRS STRT is displayed, open the door, place the pan in the unit. Close the door and select START/ STOP to begin cooking. 7. Flip halfway through the cooking time. Serve.

Serving Suggestions: Serve with pickle sauce.
Variation Tip: You can use cream instead of mayonnaise.
Nutritional Information per Serving:
Calories: 81 | Fat: 3.5g | Sat Fat: 0.6g | Carbohydrates: 8.4g | Fiber: 0.8g | Sugar: 1.9g | Protein: 5g

Crispy Sea Scallops

Prep Time: 10 minutes | Cook Time: 7 minutes | Servings: 2

 Ingredients:

1 large egg
⅓ cup potato flakes, mashed
⅛ teaspoon salt
⅛ teaspoon pepper

6 sea scallops
2 tablespoons all-purpose flour
Cooking oil

Preparation:

1. Place potato flakes in a bowl and season with salt and pepper. 2. Whisk the egg in another bowl. Place flour in a third bowl. 3. Coat the scallops with flour, then dip in egg, and finally roll in the potato mixture. 4. Arrange the scallops in the Pro-Heat Pan and spray with oil. 5. Install the Accessory Frame in top level of the oven, then place the Pro-Heat Pan on top of it. Close the door. 6. Select BROIL. Set the temperature to 400°F and set the time to 7 minutes. Press START/STOP to begin cooking, tossing them in between. 7. Dish out and serve.

Serving Suggestions: Serve with any sauce.
Variation Tip: You can also add cheese.
Nutritional Information per Serving:
Calories: 298 |Fat: 5g|Sat Fat: 1g|Carbohydrates: 33g|Fiber: 2g|Sugar: 2g|Protein: 28g

Simple Egg Yolks with Squid

Prep Time: 15 minutes | Cook Time: 18 minutes | Servings: 4

 Ingredients:

½ cup self-rising flour
14 ounces squid flower, cleaned and pat dried
Salt and black pepper
1 tablespoon olive oil
2 tablespoons butter
2 green chilies, seeded and chopped

2 curry leaves stalks
4 raw salted egg yolks
½ cup chicken broth
2 tablespoons evaporated milk
1 tablespoon sugar

 Preparation:

1. Place the flour in a shallow bowl. 2. Sprinkle the squid flower with salt and pepper. 3. Coat the squid evenly with flour and then shake off any excess. Place the squid in the Pro-Heat Pan. 4. Install the Accessory Frame in the bottom of the oven, then place the Pro-Heat Pan on top of it. Close the door. 5. Select BROIL. Set the temperature to 425°F and set the time to 10 minutes. Press START/STOP to begin cooking, tossing once in between. 6. Meanwhile, in a skillet over medium heat, add the oil and butter and sauté the chilies and curry leaves for about 3 minutes. 7. Whisk in the egg yolks and cook for about 1 minute, stirring continuously. 8. Pour in the chicken broth gradually and cook for about 5 minutes, stirring continuously. 9. Add in the milk and sugar and stir to mix well. 10. Add the broiled squid and toss until well coated. 11. Serve warm.

Serving Suggestions: Serve topped with the sour cream and smoked salmon slices.
Variation Tip: You can use red potatoes too.
Nutritional Information per Serving:
Calories: 320| Fat: 16.6g|Sat Fat: 6.2g|Carbohydrates: 19.9g|Fiber: 0.8g|Sugar: 4.2g|Protein: 20.7g

Spicy Moroccan Fish

Prep Time: 15 minutes | Cook Time: 15 minutes | Servings: 12

 Ingredients:

1 tablespoon vegetable oil
1 onion, chopped
1 clove garlic, chopped
1 can garbanzo beans, drained and rinsed
2 bell peppers, slices, and seeded
1 carrot, sliced
3 tomatoes, chopped
4 olives, chopped

¼ cup parsley, chopped
¼ cup ground cumin
3 tablespoons paprika
1 teaspoon cayenne pepper
Salt, to taste
2 tablespoons chicken bouillon granules
5 pounds tilapia fillets

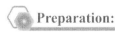 **Preparation:**

1. Combine all ingredients in the Pro-Heat Pan and shower with cooking oil spray. 2. Install the Accessory Frame in top level of the oven, then place the Pro-Heat Pan on top of it. Close the door. 3. Select BROIL. Set the temperature to 425°F and set the time to 15 minutes. Press START/STOP to begin cooking, turning them in between. 4. Serve and enjoy!

Serving Suggestions: Serve with fries or rice.
Variation Tip: You can add dried basil leaves.
Nutritional Information per Serving:
Calories: 268.2|Fat: 5.1g|Sat Fat: 0.9g|Carbohydrates: 12.6g|Fiber: 3.3g|Sugar: 3.3g|Protein: 41.7g

Lime Fish Tacos

Prep Time: 10 minutes | Cook Time: 10 minutes | Servings: 3

 Ingredients:

12 ounces cod, cut into ½ inch
1 teaspoon salt, divided
½ lime
½ cup all-purpose flour
1 large egg, lightly beaten
1 cup bread crumbs

½ cup avocado
3 whole-wheat tortillas
½ cup cabbage, shredded
½ cup cilantro, roughly chopped
½ cup sour cream
Lime wedges, to serve

 Preparation:

1. Season cod with ½ teaspoon salt and drizzle with lime juice. 2. Place flour in a bowl; whisk the egg in a second bowl; combine the breadcrumbs and salt in a third bowl. 3. Roll the cod in the flour and shake off any excess, then dip it into the egg, and finally coat it in the bread crumbs. 4. Arrange the coated cod in the Pro-Heat Pan and spray with oil. 5. Install the Accessory Frame in top level of the oven, then place the Pro-Heat Pan on top of it. Close the door. 6. Select BROIL. Set the temperature to 400°F and set the time to 10 minutes. Press START/STOP to begin cooking, tossing them in between. 7. Then heat the tortillas on a pan for about 2 minutes. 8. Serve tacos with two fish pieces, and add cabbage, cilantro, avocado, sour cream, and lime.

Serving Suggestions: You can serve with mustard sauce on top.
Variation Tip: You can use cheese cream instead of sour cream.
Nutritional Information per Serving:
Calories: 552|Fat: 18.2g|Sat Fat: 7.3g|Carbohydrates: 58.3g|Fiber: 6g|Sugar: 3.4g|Protein: 38.3g

Crispy Calamari

Prep Time: 10 minutes | Cook Time: 5 minutes | Servings: 6

 Ingredients:

1-pound calamari tubes, thawed
Kosher salt to taste
½ cup 2% milk
1½ cups all-purpose flour
⅓ cup cornstarch

½ teaspoon baking powder
½ teaspoon black pepper
½ teaspoon cayenne pepper
½ teaspoon oregano
Grape seed oil, as required

 Preparation:

1. Slice the calamari tubes into thick rings. 2. In a bowl, mix ½ cup milk and salt. 3. Add the calamari rings to the milk mixture and marinate for 30 minutes. 4. In a large bowl, mix together the flour, cornstarch, baking powder, peppers and oregano. 5. Roll the calamari rings in the flour mixture. 6. Arrange the calamari rings in the Pro-Heat Pan and spray with oil. 7. Install the Accessory Frame in top level of the oven, then place the Pro-Heat Pan on top of it. Close the door. 8. Select BROIL. Set the temperature to 375°F and set the time to 5 minutes. Press START/STOP to begin cooking, tossing them in between. 9. When done, season with salt and serve warm.

Serving Suggestions: Serve with lemon wedges.
Variation Tip: You can add white pepper.
Nutritional Information per Serving:
Calories: 227| Fat: 1.8g|Sat Fat: 0.6g|Carbohydrates: 35.8g|Fiber: 1.6g|Sugar: 0.2g|Protein: 15.9g

Butter Crumb-Topped Sole

Prep Time: 10 minutes | Cook Time: 8 minutes | Servings: 4

Ingredients:

3 tablespoons reduced-fat mayonnaise
3 tablespoons parmesan cheese, grated, divided
2 teaspoons mustard seed
¼ teaspoon pepper
4 sole fillets

1 cup soft bread crumbs
1 green onion, finely chopped
½ teaspoon ground mustard
2 teaspoons butter, melted

Preparation:

1. In a bowl, combine the mayonnaise, mustard seed, 2 tablespoons cheese, and pepper. Stir to mix well. Then spread this mixture over the tops of fillets. 2. Arrange the fillets in the Pro-Heat Pan and spray with cooking oil. 3. Install the Accessory Frame in top level of the oven, then place the Pro-Heat Pan on top of it. Close the door. 4. Select BROIL. Set the temperature to 425°F and set the time to 5 minutes. Press START/STOP to begin cooking, tossing them in between. 5. Meanwhile, mix together the bread crumbs, ground mustard, onion, butter and remaining cheese in a bowl. 6. Spread the mixture over the fillets, and broil for 3 minutes more. 7. Sprinkle with onions and serve.

Serving Suggestions: Serve with fries.
Variation Tip: You can use any cheese.
Nutritional Information per Serving:
Calories: 267 | Fat: 10g|Sat Fat: 3g|Carbohydrates: 8g|Fiber: 1g|Sugar: 1g|Protein: 35g

Salmon Fillet with Salsa

Prep Time: 10 minutes | Cook Time: 8 minutes | Servings: 1

Ingredients:

For Salsa:
¼ cup red bell pepper, seeded and chopped
1 tablespoon red onion, chopped
½ cup fresh pineapple chopped
For Salmon:
½ tablespoon extra-virgin olive oil
1 tablespoon fresh cilantro leaves, chopped
1 salmon fillets

½ tablespoon fresh lemon juice
Fresh ground black pepper to taste

Pinch of salt
Fresh ground black pepper to taste

Preparation:

1. In a bowl, combine all the salsa ingredients. 2. Season the salmon with salt and black pepper and place in the Pro-Heat Pan and shower with olive oil. 3. Install the Accessory Frame in the bottom of the oven, then place the Pro-Heat Pan on top of it. Close the door. 4. While holding the smoke box open, use the pellet scoop to pour pellets into the smoke box until filled to the top. Then close the smoke box. 5. Turn dial to select SMOKER, set the temperature to 450°F, and set the time to 8 minutes. Select START/STOP to begin cooking. Flip halfway through the cooking time. 6. When cook time is complete, divide salsa onto both plates alongside salmon fillets and sprinkle with chopped cilantro leaves. Serve and enjoy!

Serving Suggestions: Serve lemon on the side and garnish with parsley.
Variation Tip: Cook the salmon until it is flaky and still pink on the inside.
Nutritional Information per Serving:
Calories: 338 | Fat: 18.2g | Sat Fat: 2.6g | Carbohydrates: 10.4g | Fiber: 1.2g | Sugar: 7.1g | Protein: 35.5g

Balsamic Baked Salmon with Garlic

Prep Time: 10 minutes | Cook Time: 30 minutes | Servings: 8

Ingredients:

1 cup balsamic vinegar

¼ cup quality dark honey

4 garlic cloves, minced

½ teaspoon cayenne pepper

½ teaspoon Aleppo pepper

3 tablespoons Dijon mustard

2 tablespoons extra virgin olive oil

3 lb. salmon fillet, no skin

Salt to taste

Pepper to taste

⅓ cup parsley leaves, chopped

⅓ cup fresh dill, chopped

Preparation:

1. In a saucepan over medium heat, add the honey and balsamic vinegar and let it simmer. Cook for around 15 minutes. 2. Then stir in the garlic, oil, spices, and mustard. Mix well. 3. Season both sides of the salmon with salt and pepper. 4. Brush the salmon with the honey mixture and arrange them in the Pro-Heat Pan. 5. Install the Accessory Frame in the bottom level of the unit. Turn left-hand dial to select BAKE. Set the temperature to 400°F and set the time to 15 minutes. Select START/STOP to begin preheating. 6. When unit is preheated and ADD FOOD and PRS STRT is displayed, open the door, place the pan in the unit. Close the door and select START/ STOP to begin cooking. 7. Take out and serve.

Serving Suggestions: Serve with chopped parsley and dill on top.

Variation Tip: You can add crushed red chilies to add some spice.

Nutritional Information per Serving:

Calories: 211 | Fat: 8.3g | Sat Fat: 1.6g | Carbohydrates: 8g | Fiber: 3.5g | Sugar: 4.9g | Protein: 25.6g

Chapter 7 Dessert Recipes

Chocolate Lava Cake

Prep Time: 15 minutes | Cook Time: 12 minutes | Servings: 4

 **Ingredients:**

⅔ cup chocolate chips

½ cup unsalted butter, softened

2 large eggs

2 large egg yolks

1 cup confectioners' sugar

1 teaspoon peppermint extract

⅓ cup all-purpose flour plus more for dusting

2 tablespoons powdered sugar

⅓ cup fresh raspberries

 **Preparation:**

1. Install the Accessory Frame in the bottom level of the unit. Turn the left-hand dial to select BAKE. Set the temperature to 375°F and set the time to 12 minutes. Select START/STOP to begin preheating. 2. Microwave chocolate chips and butter on high for about 30 seconds. Mix well. 3. Whisk in eggs, powdered sugar, peppermint extract, confectioners' sugar and egg yolks until well combined. 4. Add flour and gently stir to combine. 5. Butter 4 ramekins and dust each with a bit of flour. 6. Place the mixture evenly into the prepared ramekins. Then place the ramekins into the Pro-Heat Pan. 7. When unit is preheated and ADD FOOD and PRS STRT is displayed, open the door, and place the pan in the unit. Close the door and select START/ STOP to begin cooking. 8. When cook time is complete, place the ramekins on a wire rack to cool for about 5 minutes. 9. Run a spatula around the edges of the ramekins to loosen the cakes. 10. Invert each cake onto a dessert plate and sprinkle with powdered sugar. 11. Garnish with fresh raspberries and serve.

Serving Suggestions: Serve with vanilla ice cream and cherry sauce.
Variation Tip: You can also use fresh fruits with the lava cake.
Nutritional Information per Serving:
Calories: 424 | Fat: 24.1g | Sat Fat: 14.7g | Carbohydrates: 47.5g | Fiber: 1.1g | Sugar: 12.9g | Protein: 4.8g

Classic Shortbread Fingers

Prep Time: 15 minutes | Cook Time: 12 minutes | Servings: 10

 **Ingredients:**

⅓ cup caster sugar

1⅔ cups plain flour

¾ cup butter

 **Preparation:**

1. Install the Accessory Frame in the bottom level of the unit. Turn left-hand dial to select BAKE. Set the temperature to 355°F and set the time to 12 minutes. Select START/STOP to begin preheating. 2. Combine the flour, sugar, and butter in a bowl. Mix until a smooth dough forms. 3. Cut the dough into 10 equal-sized fingers and lightly prick the fingers with a fork. 4. Lightly grease the Pro-Heat Pan and arrange fingers in a single layer. 5. When unit is preheated and ADD FOOD and PRS STRT is displayed, open the door, place the pan in the unit. Close the door and select START/ STOP to begin cooking. 6. Remove the shortbreads and allow them to cool for about 5-10 minutes. Serve.

Serving Suggestions: Serve with tea.
Variation Tip: You can use gluten-free flour.
Nutritional Information per Serving:
Calories: 223 | Fat: 14g | Sat Fat: 8.8g | Carbohydrates: 22.6g | Fiber: 0.6g | Sugar: 6.7g | Protein: 2.3g

Yummy Raisin Bread Pudding

Prep Time: 15 minutes | Cook Time: 12 minutes | Servings: 4

 Ingredients:

1 cup milk

1 egg

1 tablespoon brown sugar

½ teaspoon ground cinnamon

¼ teaspoon vanilla extract

2 tablespoons raisins, soaked in hot water for about 15 minutes

2 bread slices, cut into small cubes

1 tablespoon chocolate chips

1 tablespoon sugar

 Preparation:

1. In a bowl, mix together the milk, egg, brown sugar, cinnamon, and vanilla extract; stir in the raisins. 2. In the Pro-Heat Pan, spread the bread cubes and pour the milk mixture evenly on top. 3. Refrigerate for about 15-20 minutes. 4. Install the Accessory Frame in the bottom level of the unit. Turn left-hand dial to select BAKE. Set the temperature to 375°F and set the time to 12 minutes. Select START/STOP to begin preheating. 5. When unit is preheated and ADD FOOD and PRS STRT is displayed, open the door, place the pan in the unit. Sprinkle with chocolate chips and sugar on top. Close the door and select START/ STOP to begin cooking. 6. Serve warm.

Serving Suggestions: Serve with whipped cream or cream cheese frosting.
Variation Tip: You can add walnuts as well.
Nutritional Information per Serving:
Calories: 119 | Fat: 3.4g | Sat Fat: 1.7g | Carbohydrates: 18.3g | Fiber: 0.6g | Sugar: 12.4g | Protein: 4.4g

Delectable Fruity Crumble

Prep Time: 15 minutes | Cook Time: 20 minutes | Servings: 6

 Ingredients:

1 cup all-purpose flour

½ cup fresh blackberries

⅓ cup sugar, divided

1 tablespoon fresh lemon juice

1 fresh apricot, pitted and cubed

Pinch of salt

1 tablespoon cold water

¼ cup chilled butter, cubed

Preparation:

1. In a large bowl, combine the apricots, blackberries, 2 tablespoons of sugar, and lemon juice. Stir to mix well. 2. Spread the fruit mixture into the greased Pro-Heat Pan. 3. In another bowl, mix the flour with the remaining sugar, butter, salt and water. Stir until the mixture becomes crumbly. 4. Spread the flour mixture evenly over the fruit mixture. 5. Install the Accessory Frame in top level of the oven, then place the Pro-Heat Pan on top of it. Close the door. 6. Select BROIL. Set the temperature to 390°F and set the time to 20 minutes. Press START/STOP to begin cooking. 7. Remove from the oven and serve warm.

Serving Suggestions: Serve with fresh whipped cream and raspberries.
Variation Tip: You can use brown sugar.
Nutritional Information per Serving:
Calories: 291 | Fat: 12g | Sat Fat: 7.4g | Carbohydrates: 43.3g | Fiber: 2g | Sugar: 18.5g | Protein: 3.7g

Tasty Chocolate Mug cake

Prep Time: 15 minutes | Cook Time: 13 minutes | Servings: 1

 Ingredients:

¼ cup self-rising flour
5 tablespoons caster sugar
1 tablespoon cocoa powder

3 tablespoons coconut oil
3 tablespoons whole milk

Preparation:

1. Install the Accessory Frame in the bottom level of the unit. Turn left-hand dial to select BAKE. Set the temperature to 390°F and set the time to 13 minutes. Select START/STOP to begin preheating. 2. Combine all the ingredients in a shallow mug and stir to mix well. 3. Place the mug in the Pro-Heat Pan. 4. When unit is preheated and ADD FOOD and PRS STRT is displayed, open the door, place the pan in the unit. Close the door and select START/ STOP to begin cooking. 5. Once done, remove from the oven and serve warm.

Serving Suggestions: Top with chocolate ganache and mini marshmallows
Variation Tip: You can substitute chocolate for cocoa powder
Nutritional Information per Serving:
Calories: 536 | Fat: 43.3g | Sat Fat: 36.6g | Carbohydrates: 37.2g | Fiber: 2.5g | Sugar: 11g | Protein: 5.7g

Baked Pumpkin Streusel Pie Bars

Prep Time: 15 minutes | Cook Time: 45 minutes | Servings: 16

 Ingredients:

1¾ cups all-purpose flour
⅔ cup quick-cooking oats
⅔ cup light brown sugar, firmly packed
1 cup cold butter, diced
1 (16-ounce) can of pumpkin

1 (14-ounce) can condensed milk, sweetened
1½ teaspoons pumpkin pie spice
1 teaspoon salt, divided
1 teaspoon lemon zest
2 large eggs

 Preparation:

1. Install the Accessory Frame in the bottom level of the unit. Turn left-hand dial to select BAKE. Set the temperature to 350°F and set the time to 10 minutes. Select START/STOP to begin preheating. 2. Line the Pro-Heat Pan with parchment paper. 3. In a large bowl, combine the flour, brown sugar, oats, and ½ teaspoon salt. Add the butter and mix until the mixture becomes crumbly. 4. Gently press the mixture into the bottom of the pan. 5. When unit is preheated and ADD FOOD and PRS STRT is displayed, open the door, place the pan in the unit. Close the door and select START/ STOP to begin cooking. 6. Once done, let it cool for 30 minutes. 7. In a large bowl, mix together the pumpkin, eggs, condensed milk, lemon zest, pumpkin pie spice, and remaining ½ teaspoon salt. Pour the mixture over the cooled crust. 8. Bake in the oven until the filling is set, about 35 minutes. 9. Let it cool completely and refrigerate for about 4 hours. 10. Cut into squares and serve.

Serving Suggestions: Serve with whipped cream or mascarpone cheese.
Variation Tip: You can use cinnamon powder as well.
Nutritional Information per Serving:
Calories: 337 | Fat: 14.9g | Sat Fat: 9g | Carbohydrates: 46g | Fiber: 2g | Sugar: 22.7g | Protein: 6.3g

Peach and Berry Pizza

Prep Time: 10 minutes | Cook Time: 15 minutes | Servings: 8

 Ingredients:

1 (1-pound) package of refrigerated pizza dough
3 tablespoons honey
¼ teaspoon fresh orange zest
2 ounces cream cheese, softened
1 (8-ounce) package crème fraîche

1 tablespoon of fresh orange juice
⅛ teaspoon ground cinnamon
1 peach, halved, pitted
1 cup blackberries
1 cup raspberries

 Preparation:

1. Install the Accessory Frame in the bottom level of the unit. Turn left-hand dial to select BAKE. Set the temperature to 400°F and set the time to 10 minutes. Select START/STOP to begin preheating. 2. Grease the Pro-Heat Pan with oil. Roll the dough into a 10-inch circle and place in the pan. 3. When unit is preheated and ADD FOOD and PRS STRT is displayed, open the door, place the pan in the unit. Close the door and select START/ STOP to begin cooking. 4. Once it's done, remove from the oven and set it aside. 5. Place cream cheese in a bowl and whisk until smooth. Add in crème fraîche, orange zest, juice, honey, and cinnamon, beating until well combined. Refrigerate until ready to use. 6. Place the peach slices in the Pro-Heat Pan and broil at 380°F for 5 minutes until softened. 7. Spread crème fraîche mixture onto the warm crust and top with peach slices, raspberries and blackberries. 8. Cut into slices and serve!

Serving Suggestions: Garnish with fresh mint leaves and honey.
Variation Tip: You can use any variety of fruits.
Nutritional Information per Serving:
Calories: 206 |Fat: 6.1g|Sat Fat: 1.6g|Carbohydrates: 36.3g|Fiber: 4.4g|Sugar: 10g|Protein: 5.2g

Stuffed Apples with Sauce

Prep Time: 15 minutes | Cook Time: 13 minutes | Servings: 4

 Ingredients:

For Stuffed Apples:
4 small firm apples, cored
½ cup golden raisins
For Vanilla Sauce:
½ cup whipped cream
2 tablespoons sugar

2 tablespoons sugar
½ cup blanched almonds

½ teaspoon vanilla extract

 Preparation:

1. Install the Accessory Frame in the bottom level of the unit. Turn left-hand dial to select BAKE. Set the temperature to 355°F and set the time to 10 minutes. Select START/STOP to begin preheating. 2. Add raisins, almonds, and sugar to a food processor and pulse until chopped. 3. Stuff each apple with the raisin mixture and arrange them in the Pro-Heat Pan. 4. When unit is preheated and ADD FOOD and PRS STRT is displayed, open the door, place the pan in the unit. Close the door and select START/ STOP to begin cooking. 5. Meanwhile, in a pan, add the cream, vanilla extract and sugar and cook until the sugar is dissolved, stirring continuously. 6. Once the apples are done, remove from the oven and place the apples onto serving plates to cool slightly. 7. Add the vanilla sauce on top and serve.

Serving Suggestions: Top with cream cheese frosting.
Variation Tip: You can use cinnamon and brown sugar.
Nutritional Information per Serving:
Calories: 329 | Fat: 11.1g | Sat Fat: 3.4g | Carbohydrates: 60.2g | Fiber: 7.6g | Sugar: 46.5g | Protein: 4g

Mini Baked Apple Pies

Prep Time: 20 minutes | Cook Time: 30 minutes | Servings: 6

 **Ingredients:**

For Crust:

1½ cups flour

1 teaspoon sugar

½ cup unsalted butter

¼ cup chilled water

Salt, to taste

For Filling:

4 Granny Smith apples, peeled and finely chopped

1 teaspoon fresh lemon zest, finely grated

1 teaspoon ground cinnamon

¼ teaspoon ground nutmeg

2½ tablespoons sugar

2 tablespoons flour

Salt, to taste

2 tablespoons fresh lemon juice

2 tablespoons butter

For Topping:

1 egg, beaten

1 teaspoon ground cinnamon

3 tablespoons sugar

 **Preparation:**

1. For the crust: In a bowl, combine the flour, butter, sugar, and salt. Pour in the chilled water and mix until a dough forms. Cover the bowl with plastic wrap and refrigerate for about 30 minutes. 2. For the filling: Combine all the filling ingredients in a large bowl and set aside. 3. For the topping: In a third bowl, whisk together the beaten egg, cinnamon, and sugar. 4. Roll out dough to ½-inch thickness. Using a ramekin, cut 12 circles from dough. 5. Place 6 circles in bottom of 6 ramekins; press down slightly. 6. Divide filling mixture among each ramekin and top with remaining circles. 7. Pinch edges together to seal the pies. 8. Carefully cut 3 small slits in each pastry; coat evenly with beaten egg. 9. Sprinkle each pie with cinnamon sugar mixture. 10. Arrange the ramekins into the Pro-Heat Pan. 11. Install the Accessory Frame in the bottom level of the unit. Turn left-hand dial to select BAKE. Set the temperature to 350°F and set the time to 30 minutes. Select START/STOP to begin preheating. 12. When unit is preheated and ADD FOOD and PRS STRT is displayed, open the door, place the pan in the unit. Close the door and select START/ STOP to begin cooking. 13. Once done, remove the ramekins and let them cool for about 10-15 minutes. Serve warm.

Serving Suggestions: Drizzle salted caramel sauce.

Variation Tip: You can skip the lemon zest.

Nutritional Information per Serving:

Calories: 442 | Fat: 22.6g | Sat Fat: 2.1g | Carbohydrates: 58.2g | Fiber: 9g | Sugar: 29.2g | Protein: 5.2g

Butter Chocolate Soufflé

Prep Time: 15 minutes | Cook Time: 16 minutes | Servings: 2

 **Ingredients:**

3 ounces semi-sweet chocolate, chopped
½ teaspoon pure vanilla extract
2 tablespoons all-purpose flour
¼ cup butter

2 eggs, egg yolks, and whites separated
3 tablespoons sugar
1 teaspoon powdered sugar plus extra for dusting

 **Preparation:**

1. In a microwave-safe bowl, combine butter and chocolate. Microwave on high for about 2 minutes, until completely melted, stirring every 30 seconds. 2. Remove from microwave and whisk mixture until smooth. 3. In another bowl, whisk together egg yolks, vanilla extract and sugar. 4. Add chocolate mixture, whisking until completely blended. 5. Gently fold in flour to mixture, whisking to combine. 6. In a separate bowl, whip egg whites until soft peaks form. 7. Fold the whipped egg whites into the chocolate mixture in three portions. 8. Install the Accessory Frame in the bottom level of the unit. Turn left-hand dial to select BAKE. Set the temperature to 330°F and set the time to 14 minutes. Select START/STOP to begin preheating. 9. Lightly grease 2 ramekins and sprinkle with a pinch of sugar. 10. Place the mixture evenly into the prepared ramekins, smoothing the tops with the back of a spoon. 11. Arrange the ramekins in the Pro-Heat Pan. 12. When unit is preheated and ADD FOOD and PRS STRT is displayed, open the door, place the pan in the unit. Close the door and select START/ STOP to begin cooking. 13. Remove from the oven and set aside to cool slightly. 14. Sprinkle the powdered sugar on top and serve warm with ice cream.

Serving Suggestions: Top with some chocolate ganache.
Variation Tip: You can use dark chocolate instead of semi-sweet chocolate.
Nutritional Information per Serving:
Calories: 569 | Fat: 38.8g | Sat Fat: 23g | Carbohydrates: 54.1g | Fiber: 0.5g | Sugar: 42.4g | Protein: 6.9g

Delicious Cheesecake

Prep Time: 15 minutes | Cook Time: 35 minutes | Servings: 6

 **Ingredients:**

Crust:

1 cup Graham crackers

2 teaspoons sugar

Cheesecake:

28 oz. cream cheese

⅔ cup sugar

¼ teaspoon salt

1 teaspoon vanilla

1 teaspoon cinnamon

3 tablespoons butter

zest of lemon

2 eggs, room temp

⅔ cup sour cream

1 can cherries, for topping

 Preparation:

1. Install the Accessory Frame in the bottom level of the unit. Turn left-hand dial to select BAKE. Set the temperature to 350°F and set the time to 30 minutes. Select START/STOP to begin preheating. 2. In a bowl, mix together the graham crackers, sugar, cinnamon, and butter. 3. Press this mixture into the bottom of the Pro-Heat Pan. 4. Chill in the refrigerator for 10-15 minutes to set. 5. Combine the cream cheese, salt, sugar, lemon zest, vanilla, eggs and sour cream. Mix well until smooth. Pour into frozen crust. 6. When unit is preheated and ADD FOOD and PRS STRT is displayed, open the door, place the pan in the unit. Close the door and select START/ STOP to begin cooking. 7. When cooking time is up, turn the cook mode to "Broil" and broil for 5 minutes at 425°F. 8. Carefully remove the cheesecake and chill in the refrigerator for at least 4 hours. 9. Once completely chilled, top evenly with the cherry topping or your favorite topping and crushed graham crackers. Serve.

Serving Suggestions: You can serve it with mint leaves on top!

Variation Tip: You can add mascarpone cheese to the filling as well.

Nutritional Information per Serving:

Calories: 560|Fat: 40g|Sat Fat: 22g|Carbohydrates: 44g|Fiber: 1g|Sugar: 32g|Protein: 9g

Baked Lemon Bars

Prep Time: 15 minutes | Cook Time: 35 minutes | Servings: 12

 Ingredients:

For the Crust:

1½ cups packed almond flour, fine-blanched
2 tablespoons coconut flour
¼ teaspoon almond extract

¼ teaspoon salt
¼ cup butter, melted and cooled
¼ cup pure maple syrup

For the Filling:

Zest from 1 lemon
½ cup pure maple syrup
4 large eggs

⅔ cup lemon juice, freshly squeezed
1 tablespoon coconut flour, sifted

 Preparation:

1. Install the Accessory Frame in the bottom level of the unit. Turn left-hand dial to select BAKE. Set the temperature to 350°F and set the time to 15 minutes. Select START/STOP to begin preheating. 2. Grease the Pro-Heat Pan with butter. 3. To prepare the crust, in a mixing bowl, combine the almond flour, coconut flour and salt. 4. Add pure maple syrup, butter, and almond extract to the flour mixture; stir until well combined. 5. Form the dough with your hands and press it evenly into the prepared pan. 6. When unit is preheated and ADD FOOD and PRS STRT is displayed, open the door, place the pan in the unit. Close the door and select START/ STOP to begin cooking. 7. Meanwhile, to make the filling, whisk together the eggs, lemon zest, pure maple syrup, lemon juice, and sifted coconut flour in a bowl. 8. When the crust is baked, pour the filling into it carefully. 9. Reduce temperature to 325°F and bake for 20-25 minutes more until the filling is set and no longer jiggles. 10. Allow it to Cool on a wire rack and refrigerate for at least 4 hours. 11. Cut out 12 bars with a sharp knife and serve!

Serving Suggestions: Garnish with lemon zest.
Variation Tip: You can also use arrowroot starch instead of coconut flour.
Nutritional Information per Serving:
Calories: 84 | Fat: 4.4g | Sat Fat: 1.3g | Carbohydrates: 8g | Fiber: 1g | Sugar: 5.7g | Protein: 3.1g

Yummy Apple Bread Pudding

Prep Time: 15 minutes | Cook Time: 22 minutes | Servings: 8

 Ingredients:

For Bread Pudding:
10½ ounces bread, cubed
½ cup apple, peeled, cored, and chopped
½ cup raisins
¼ cup walnuts, chopped
1½ cups milk
For Topping:
1⅓ cups plain flour
½ cup brown sugar

¾ cup water
5 tablespoons honey
2 teaspoons ground cinnamon
2 teaspoons cornstarch
1 teaspoon vanilla extract

7 tablespoons butter

 Preparation:

1. In a large bowl, combine the bread, raisins, apples, and walnuts. 2. In another bowl, combine the remaining pudding ingredients and pour in the bread mixture. 3. Refrigerate for about 15 minutes, tossing occasionally. 4. To prepare the topping: Mix the flour and sugar in a bowl. Stir in the cold butter cubes until a crumbly mixture forms. 5. Install the Accessory Frame in the bottom level of the unit. Turn left-hand dial to select BAKE. Set the temperature to 350°F and set the time to 22 minutes. Select START/STOP to begin preheating. 6. Place the bread mixture in the Pro-Heat Pan and spread the topping mixture on top. 7. When unit is preheated and ADD FOOD and PRS STRT is displayed, open the door, place the pan in the unit. Close the door and select START/ STOP to begin cooking. 8. Remove from the oven and serve warm.

Serving Suggestions: Sprinkle powdered sugar and serve with caramel sauce.
Variation Tip: You can add a pinch of nutmeg for taste variation.
Nutritional Information per Serving:
Calories: 432 | Fat: 14.8g | Sat Fat: 2.1g | Carbohydrates: 69.1g | Fiber: 4.7g | Sugar: 32g | Protein: 7.9g

Delicious Vanilla Soufflé

Prep Time: 15 minutes | Cook Time: 30 minutes | Servings: 6

 Ingredients:

¼ cup butter, softened
¼ cup all-purpose flour
½ cup plus 2 tablespoons sugar, divided
1 cup milk
3 teaspoons vanilla extract, divided

4 egg yolks
5 egg whites
1 teaspoon cream of tartar
2 tablespoons confectioners' sugar plus extra for dusting

 Preparation:

1. In a bowl, mix the flour and butter until a smooth paste is formed. 2. In a saucepan, combine ½ cup sugar and milk and cook over low heat, stirring constantly, until the sugar is dissolved. 3. Add the flour mixture and cook, stirring constantly, for about 3-4 minutes, until the mixture is thickened. 4. Stir in 1 teaspoon of the vanilla extract. Allow to cool for 10 minutes. 5. Add egg yolks and 1 teaspoon vanilla extract to a bowl and whisk to combine. 6. Add egg yolk mixture to milk mixture and whisk until well blended. 7. In a separate bowl, combine egg whites, remaining sugar, cream of tartar, and vanilla extract, whisking until stiff peaks form. 8. Gently pour the egg white mixture into the milk mixture. 9. Install the Accessory Frame in the bottom level of the unit. Turn left-hand dial to select BAKE. Set the temperature to 330°F and set the time to 15 minutes. Select START/STOP to begin preheating. 10. Lightly grease 6 ramekins and sprinkle with a pinch of sugar. Place the mixture evenly into the prepared ramekins, smoothing the tops with the back of a spoon. 11. Place the ramekins in two batches in the Pro-Heat Pan. 12. When unit is preheated and ADD FOOD and PRS STRT is displayed, open the door, place the pan in the unit. Close the door and select START/STOP to begin cooking. 13. When done, remove from the oven and cool slightly. 14. Sprinkle with powdered sugar and serve warm.

Serving Suggestions: Serve with vanilla cookies.
Variation Tip: You can also use gluten-free flour or almond flour
Nutritional Information per Serving:
Calories: 238 | Fat: 11.6g | Sat Fat: 6.5g | Carbohydrates: 26.5g | Fiber: 0.1g | Sugar: 21.7g | Protein: 6.8g

Delicious Milky Donuts

Prep Time: 15 minutes | Cook Time: 16 minutes | Servings: 12

 **Ingredients:**

For Doughnuts:

1 cup all-purpose flour

1 cup whole wheat flour

2 teaspoons baking powder

Salt, to taste

¾ cup sugar

For Glaze:

2 tablespoons icing sugar

1 tablespoon cocoa powder

1 egg

1 tablespoon butter, softened

½ cup milk

2 teaspoons vanilla extract

2 tablespoons condensed milk

 Preparation:

1. In a large bowl, mix the flour, baking powder and salt. 2. In a separate bowl, whisk the egg and sugar until fluffy and light. 3. Add the egg mixture to the flour and stir until well combined. 4. Add the milk, butter, and vanilla extract and stir until a soft dough forms. Refrigerate the dough for about 1 hour. 5. Roll the dough to ½-inch thickness and cut into 24 small doughnuts with a small doughnut cutter. 6. Place the doughnuts in a single layer in the Pro-Heat Pan. 7. Install the Accessory Frame in the bottom level of the unit. Turn left-hand dial to select BAKE. Set the temperature to 390°F and set the time to 8 minutes. Select START/STOP to begin preheating. 8. When unit is preheated and ADD FOOD and PRS STRT is displayed, open the door, place the pan in the unit. Close the door and select START/ STOP to begin cooking. You may cook in batches. 9. Once done, transfer the doughnuts to a platter to cool completely. 10. In a small bowl, mix together the condensed milk, icing sugar and cocoa powder. 11. Spread the glaze over the doughnuts and enjoy.

Serving Suggestions: Sprinkle with sugar sprinkles and serve with coffee.

Variation Tip: You can use vanilla frosting.

Nutritional Information per Serving:

Calories: 134 | Fat: 2.1g | Sat Fat: 1.1g | Carbohydrates: 26.9g | Fiber: 0.8g | Sugar: 16.2g | Protein: 2.6g

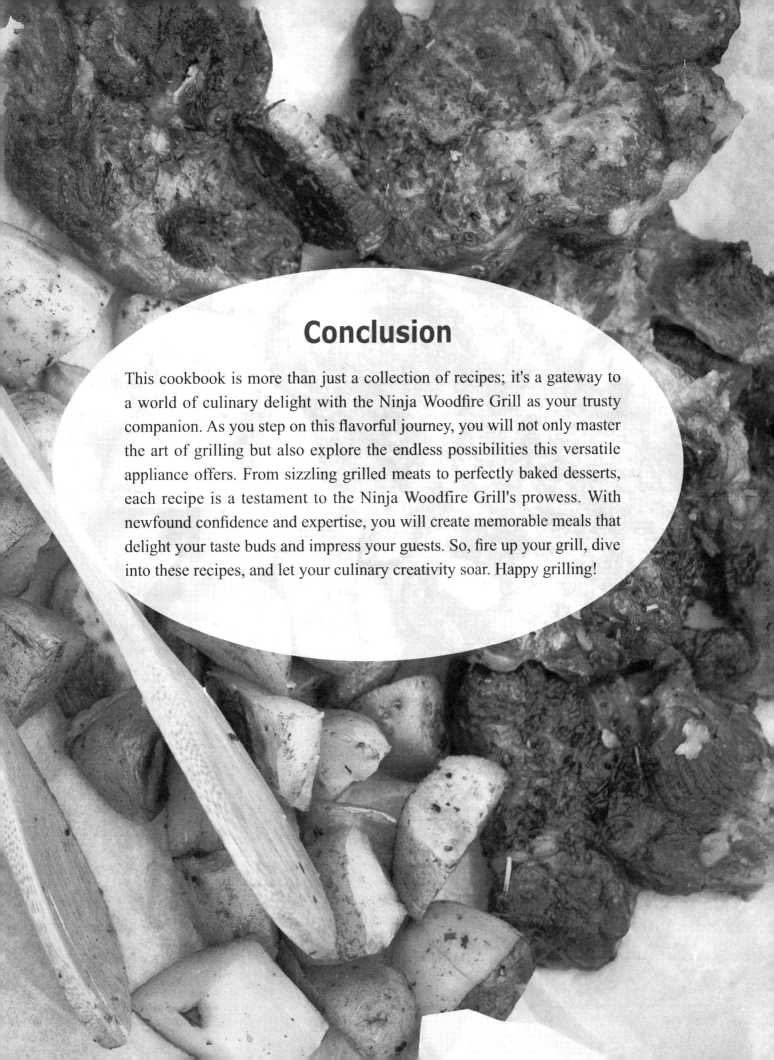

Conclusion

This cookbook is more than just a collection of recipes; it's a gateway to a world of culinary delight with the Ninja Woodfire Grill as your trusty companion. As you step on this flavorful journey, you will not only master the art of grilling but also explore the endless possibilities this versatile appliance offers. From sizzling grilled meats to perfectly baked desserts, each recipe is a testament to the Ninja Woodfire Grill's prowess. With newfound confidence and expertise, you will create memorable meals that delight your taste buds and impress your guests. So, fire up your grill, dive into these recipes, and let your culinary creativity soar. Happy grilling!

Appendix 1 Measurement Conversion Chart

WEIGHT EQUIVALENTS

US STANDARD	METRIC (APPROXINATE)
1 ounce	28 g
2 ounces	57 g
5 ounces	142 g
10 ounces	284 g
15 ounces	425 g
16 ounces(1 pound)	455 g
1. 5pounds	680 g
2pounds	907 g

VOLUME EQUIVALENTS (DRY)

US STANDARD	METRIC (APPROXIMATE)
⅛ teaspoon	0. 5 mL
¼ teaspoon	1 mL
½ teaspoon	2 mL
¾ teaspoon	4 mL
1 teaspoon	5 mL
1 tablespoon	15 mL
¼ cup	59 mL
½ cup	118 mL
¾ cup	177 mL
1 cup	235 mL
2 cups	475 mL
3 cups	700 mL
4 cups	1 L

TEMPERATURES EQUIVALENTS

FAHRENHEIT (F)	CELSIUS (C) (APPROXIMATE)
225 ℉	107 ℃
250 ℉	120 ℃
275 ℉	135 ℃
300 ℉	150 ℃
325 ℉	160 ℃
350 ℉	180 ℃
375 ℉	190 ℃
400 ℉	205 ℃
425 ℉	220 ℃
450 ℉	235 ℃
475 ℉	245 ℃
500 ℉	260 ℃

VOLUME EQUIVALENTS (LIQUID)

US STANDARD	US STANDARD (OUNCES)	METRIC (APPROXIMATE)
2 tablespoons	1 fl. oz	30 mL
¼ cup	2 fl. oz	60 mL
½ cup	4 fl. oz	120 mL
1 cup	8 fl. oz	240 mL
1½ cup	12 fl. oz	355 mL
2 cups or 1 pint	16 fl. oz	475 mL
4 cups or 1 quart	32 fl. oz	1 L
1 gallon	128 fl. oz	4 L

Appendix 2 Recipes Index

Printed in Great Britain
by Amazon